3,50

# Writers of Wales

EDITORS

MEIC STEPHENS        R. BRINLEY JONES

BOBI JONES

*(Photograph reproduced with the kind permission of the
Welsh Arts Council)*

*John Emyr*

# BOBI

# JONES

*University of Wales Press*
*on behalf of the Welsh Arts Council*

1991

14/10/91

# I

Robert Maynard Jones, best known as Bobi Jones, is perhaps the most prolific Welsh writer in the history of the language. A versatile master of poetry, fictional prose and criticism, he is now in his sixties and still producing work of a high standard at a very productive rate. Trying to write about the man and his work at this time is akin to reflecting upon a waterfall at close quarters—an awesome venture, not without its perils.

And yet, one is glad of the opportunity, difficult though the task may be, to draw a sketch or cameo, because Bobi Jones is an author of great significance, not least for non-Welsh-speakers. Having learned Welsh himself as a second language it could be argued that his work offers greater insight into the significance of the language and its culture than that of most authors whose first language is Welsh. This insight is increased by the strong intellectual and reflective element in his work.

Deeply involved with the language and its culture, passionately committed to the best things in Welsh life, there is in his work—even at

1

moments of high intensity—an element of detachment, an ability to step aside and see the wonder of Wales, its beauty and its tragedy, with an outsider's reflective, almost analytical, gaze. Perhaps this ability stems only partly from the fact that he has learned Welsh himself—a momentous but early event in his life (he was in his teens when he started to master the language). It could be that the reflective tendency, the ability to meditate and see things in a clear-eyed and integrated perspective, stems from the essence of the man as artist, thinker and committed Christian.

As a young Cardiff poet, writing his first poems and prose in the 1940s, Bobi Jones, like other Welsh writers of his generation, worked in the presence or in the wake of the Romantic old guard—T. Gwynn Jones, W. J. Gruffydd, R. Williams Parry and T. H. Parry-Williams—but, unlike some of his contemporaries who never broke through the confidence barrier, he refused to be daunted by their presence and influence. These members of the old guard, it should be remembered, had been the vanguard of the literary renaissance of the early twentieth century, and had secured for themselves a substantial degree of cultural authority. Consequently, Bobi Jones's early defiance, both in poetic style and critical comment, must have appeared to many to be disrespect bordering on insolence. He gained an early reputation for being an *enfant terrible*, the legacy of which has followed him throughout his mature years as an established and influential author and even as Professor of

2

Welsh language and literature at the University College of Wales, Aberystwyth.

Some of his juvenilia attracted deserved censure. However, an early trait, which has come to the fore periodically throughout his literary career, has been his willingness to answer back, to offer an active, unyielding, response to his critics. This habit may have intensified his image as being the bad boy of modern Welsh literature; it has certainly been a valuable asset in relation to the development of his confident stance as literary critic and parallel development as a prolific writer of creative literature.

His scope has been immense. First and foremost a poet, he has also taken a keen interest in prose, in particular the short story and the novel. Here also we see the restless, original nature of his talent. In his prose, as in his poetry, he has refused to opt contentedly for old rhythms and forms and, consequently, he has gained an unfair reputation for being a difficult writer. The charge of difficulty is partly due to the perception (he would say 'myth') that in *some* of his work—for example, some sections of his epic poem HUNLLEF ARTHUR, the second longest poem in the language—he makes few concessions to his readers; but generally the charge of difficulty is the result of the uncatholic taste of the typical Welsh reader who is often too conditioned by colonizing factors (such as a cultural inferiority complex) and too lazy to offer writers in Welsh the same effort and courtesy as would be offered writers in other European languages.

3

At first glance, Bobi Jones's life would not appear to be one of traumatic events or adventure. A secondary school Welsh teacher turned lecturer, first in education and then Welsh, and finally a professor of Welsh, a brief survey of his career shows an outwardly uneventful development, a rather typical context for a prominent twentieth-century writer in the Welsh language. A closer, less superficial, scrutiny would, perhaps, reveal a life not devoid of highlights and incidence. For instance, there was the Latin-American adventure of 1968 when he visited Mexico City, and nearly lost his life due to the unexpected effect of the high altitude on his constitution. That journey inspired one of his greatest poems (in fact, a 'sequence of poems'), 'Dieithryn ym Mecsico' (*A Stranger in Mexico*). He has also stayed for extended periods in other countries such as Quebec and Gambia, from which he usually brought home a rich cache of poems. But his most important travels have been inward adventures of reflection and his best poems—whether finding their point of departure in Mexico, Quebec or Wales—seem to generate, whatever the incidental landscape of their conception may be, their own inscapes of significance.

From his early poems onward, there has been a religious element in his work. Though full of fun and a willingness to tease, even as a young and extremely gifted schoolboy, there was always a serious side to his personality, a willingness to be open to life's metaphysical aspects. Among the many poets whom he read at an early age were Dante, Baudelaire and Blake. One names them here, not to present a simplistic theory of

4

influence, although some parallels could be found, but to show where the young Bobi Jones's interests lay. Like them, his keen awareness of the sensuous aspects of life, as witnessed, for instance, by his many poems to his wife, Beti, is constantly informed by a deep religious sensibility. This religious interest has coexisted with other interests throughout his life, before and after his conversion to Christianity in 1953. Indeed, he would claim—from his Calvinistic perspective which developed in the early sixties —that the religious sphere is the context in which the other interests of his life find their deeper meaning and significance, although he would not wish to be classified as a predominantly 'religious' poet in the narrow sense.

Another interest, or rather red-hot concern, has been his patriotism or commitment to Wales and the Welsh language. In an essay on the prose-writer D. J. Williams, he once expounded his view of the writer as a committed individual. In his attitude towards Wales, as in his attitude towards other matters of importance to him, Bobi Jones is himself a committed writer. That does not mean that his work is unduly polemic and one-dimensional. On the contrary, there is a depth and richness and complexity in his work which are often absent from the work of many writers who would claim that they are free from all shackles of commitment and conviction. Needless to say, on this account also, Bobi Jones has faced opposition as well as support, and an interesting feature of his literary criticism is the point of conflict where his basic world-view

5

comes into contact with that of other, perhaps less committed, writers and critics.

In a country whose language and culture face constant crisis, it is not surprising that some of Wales's most talented and responsible writers have offered advice and leadership. One thinks of Saunders Lewis's famous TYNGED YR IAITH *(Fate of the Language)* radio lecture in 1962 which gave rise to the Welsh Language Society. Bobi Jones too has analysed the situation and offered a strategy for saving the language. Briefly stated, the strategy he urges is to concentrate the teaching of Welsh on adults in the context of a wide and popular movement. Only such a strategy, he claims, will generate that popular and responsible support among non-Welsh-speakers so essential for the language's survival. Articles by him on this subject led, in 1984, to the creation of CYNGOR Y DYSGWYR *(Learners' Council)* now known as CYD: and his leadership and dynamic intellectual contribution in this area are widely recognized.

In the field of literary criticism, he is one of the few writers in Welsh who have given full, systematic, attention to the subject. He has written extensive critical studies, from both a popular and a specialist perspective; the latter of these perspectives is informed by his reading in structural and post-structural literary theory. Not willing to be merely a follower of literary fashions, he has worked out his own comprehensive system or theory of literature, and in his criticism, as in his poetry, novels and stories, we see the wide spectrum of his interests. Like

6

Saunders Lewis—who was an early influence—
Bobi Jones has insisted on allowing literature to
retain its life-giving contacts with life's many
aspects—the philosophical and the linguistic,
the sociological and the psychological. Consequently, there is in his criticism, as in his more
directly creative work, an impressively wide
range of interests. All in all, from the first poems
of youthful joy and daring, in Y GÂN GYNTAF, to
the long poem HUNLLEF ARTHUR, from early
short essays in criticism to later voluminous
studies, from early experiments in prose fiction
to more accomplished collections of stories, we
have here not only the most prolific but also one
of the most gifted and versatile writers that the
Welsh language has ever received during its long
and fruitful history.

Robert Maynard Jones was born on 20 May 1929
at 147 Cyfarthfa Street, Roath, Cardiff, into a
working-class family. His father, Sydney V. Jones
(1900–56) came from Merthyr Tudful, and his
mother, M. Edith Jones, née Francis, (1904–81),
had also lived in the same town. Sydney Jones's
roots, on his mother's side, were in Brecknock-
shire (his father was from Boncath); and the
family was proud of the fact that they were
descendants of Howel Harris (the pioneering
Welsh Methodist enthusiast) on one side, and
Oliver Cromwell on the other. Sydney Jones was
one of six children, and it was noted in the
family that the first letters of the names of the
first five gave a significant acronym: *W*il, *A*nn,
*L*il, *E*unice, *S*yd. The young Bobi Jones used
to say, with characteristic roguishness, that,

when his father's young brother, Glyn, was born, his grandparents had then started on GLAMORGAN!

This family lived in the same street as the author Glyn Jones, and the two Glyn Joneses were friends. Sydney Jones had left grammar school when he was about thirteen years of age to work in a coal-mine; then, after marrying, he went to work in a drapery shop in Cardiff, namely Hope Brothers in St Mary Street.

Bobi Jones's mother was the eldest of four children. She had been a nurse before her marriage. Bobi was the elder of her two sons, his brother, Keith, being two years younger. Her father, known in the family as Grandpa Francis, was a significant influence on his grandson, Bobi. Although Grandpa Francis's family roots were in Pembrokeshire, he had been brought up in Pontypridd and had worked as a railwayman for most of his life. He was a Marxist socialist, and grandfather and grandson would talk with great enthusiasm about socialist ideals, issues of the day, Mahatma Gandhi, and books. That was during the war years in 44 Bryn-glas, in Peny-darren, Merthyr Tudful, where Bobi frequently went for holidays. Grandpa Francis was a great talker, and they got on very well together. Without doubt, those happy hours of listening, conversing and learning to think in a radical way, were to be a deep and abiding influence as the autobiographical poem 'Tad-cu ac Ŵyr' (*Grandfather and Grandson*) demonstrates.

Although Grandpa Francis could speak Welsh as a child, he did not speak Welsh to Bobi; and it is an arresting fact that Bobi Jones's most intimate family circle could not speak the language either. His father's parents could speak Welsh, but Sydney Jones could not construct a sentence, although he knew some individual words. Bobi's mother, and her mother also, were equally deprived of the language. His great grandmother, on his mother's side of the family, was French; a fact which immediately reminds us of Emrys ap Iwan who had similar French connections. His brother does not speak Welsh; he has two children and the eldest grandson attends a Welsh school.

When Bobi Jones was about six or seven years old, the family moved to 9 Gelli-gaer Street, Cathays, Cardiff. It was here that he lived throughout his school and college years, apart from a year of postgraduate study in Dublin in 1950. The nearest secondary school to his home was Cathays High School, and this is the school he attended between 1940 and 1946. Here he was offered a choice between Spanish and Welsh. He wanted to opt for Spanish but was 'encouraged' to take Welsh. This is how he described, with typical humour (in PLANET 2, November 1970), that dramatic moment in his life and, we may add, in the life of Welsh literature:

*There were ninety of us, and he* [the headmaster] *asked those who wished to 'do' Welsh to stand forward. Some five quivering schoolboys ventured a step. The rest of us stood our ground, certain that Spanish would be intensely useful for our commercial weekend trips to South America later on.*

9

*And would we not have chosen Timbuktuish, if such a language existed, rather than degrade ourselves to do that indeed-to-goodness stuff?*

*But the headmaster had his job to do, and needed a 'stream': at a push, twenty-five might do, but certainly not five. It was wartime, and volunteering was in the air. 'Tell me, my boy', said he, turning on a fat blushing specimen in the middle of the front row, 'why don't you want to do Welsh?'*

*'I know enough, sir'.*

*Had I not done it in the elementary?*

*'Well, tell me, my boy. What's "good morning" in Welsh?'*

*This was one of those phrases that had somehow slipped the syllabus of the elementary. The blush reached my knees.*

*'Tell me, my boy. What's "good night"?'*

*This too had slipped attention. The blush rattled to the floor.*

*'Don't you think you'd better reconsider your decision?'*

*The vision had come.*

His Welsh teacher was W. C. Elvet Thomas, and his debt to this man has been expressed on numerous occasions. It was this teacher who gave him back what was rightfully his—the vibrant, historical language of his own people. Elvet Thomas taught the language in the context of the totality of life in this part of the world. With each new Welsh word that he learnt, the growing boy gained, unconsciously, more knowledge of his own country, a deeper awareness of his cultural environment. In other words, it was Elvet Thomas who awoke in him a love for the language which was (as the distinguished pupil said in later life):

10

*not just a means of communication, and certainly not a school subject. It was the expression of a complete national life and was linked to place-names, the Urdd, mountains and history, poetry and songs, dances and drama and the Eisteddfod, altars, and lots of enthralling Welsh characters and anecdotes.*

Little wonder that Elvet Thomas (in a recent letter to the present author) remembers his past pupil as being:

*very able and versatile. He saw the humorous side of things, a characteristic which is reflected in his contributions to the school's magazine, 'Ymlaen'. He wrote them in Welsh and English. He was in his element in the school's Eisteddfodau and he swept the board, winning everything in the literary section. He could recite in Welsh, English and French and win . . . He was also an excellent actor in Welsh drama.*

Bobi Jones's exceptional ability soon became apparent to the other members of his family. They were very proud of his achievements during his last years in Cathays High School. His cousin Geoffrey Thomas (their mothers were sisters), who later studied at Westminster Seminary in Philadelphia and became a Reformed minister and associate editor of the international Christian magazine THE BANNER OF TRUTH, remembers this period well:

*Bobi was flavour of the month during his last years in Cathays High School; top of the form, carrying off all the prizes, winning everything at the School Eisteddfodau—not only Welsh and English literary prizes but painting (a picture Bobi painted of a horse pulling a cart was on the front room wall for years—it seemed to me to be like a Constable!), and*

11

*music (he played the piano). He was the most able boy to have attended the school for years.*

However, although he was by then able to read Welsh, and write it less fluently, Bobi Jones did not yet speak the language with anyone. This was mostly due to the artificial examination emphasis on written answers. The important bridge to oral fluency was crossed during his first term (1946–7) at the University College, Cardiff, with the help of altruistic students, most of whom came from rural Wales. What finally clinched matters (after a year's study at the University College) was a stay in a farm at Bancffosfelen in the Gwendraeth Valley (Carmarthenshire) where he was captivated and enchanted by a warm and welcoming Welsh-speaking society and milieu.

The ancient language thrived anew in the unusually joyous and high-spirited personality of the young poet. In outward behaviour, during his college days, he gained some reputation for the occasional prank and frolic, which are particularly remembered or misremembered in relation to Inter-College Eisteddfodau.

His academic studies were conducted under the care and tuition of three very gifted scholars—Professor Griffith John Williams, T. J. Morgan and A. O. H. Jarman. They were to be a lasting influence, particularly in relation to his academic work. With their help and inspiration, he worked diligently and gained his BA first class honours in Welsh in 1949.

12

It was about this time (1948–9) that he met his future wife, Anne Elizabeth James—Beti—a beautiful brunette from Clunderwen, Pembrokeshire. Her father, John James, was a blacksmith and came from Arberth. He had learnt Welsh as a second language. Her mother, Gwen (née Bowen), came from Llanfallteg and was a descendant of the family of the composer and singer of ballads, Levi Gibbon.

Bobi and Beti began courting on 24 June 1949. Falling in love with Beti was a momentous event which had a great influence on his development as a poet. She is a prominent figure in many of his early and later poems, and the depth and joy of their love is celebrated throughout his literary career. Most of his books have been dedicated to her, and anyone who reads his poetry will soon discover the centrality of Beti as inspiration to his muse. To be the successful partner of a prolific author probably requires prolific gifts, a particular type of dedication and love; Beti possessed those gifts to an unusual degree. As wife, mother and homemaker, she was to provide a faithful, warm and intelligent base and support for all his academic and literary activities, a 'help meet' in every sense.

In spite of his new-found love, the aspiring scholar spent the following year in Aberystwyth and the next in Dublin, thus completing two years research work (between 1949–51) on the medieval Welsh romance OWAIN A LUNED for which he was awarded, in due course, the degree of MA. By now he was committed not only to the Welsh language but also to Wales as a politi-

cal entity. He joined Plaid Cymru in 1950. After
returning from Dublin to Wales, he took a
Diploma in Education and was then appointed
head of the Welsh department at Llanidloes High
School. Receiving a salary for the first time, the
way was now open for him to marry Beti, and
their marriage took place on 27 December 1952.

Although they lived in Llanidloes (right at the
centre of Wales) for only two years, this was an
extremely formative period, particularly because
of one event: it was here, one Sunday evening
in 1953 in a seat at the back of China Street
chapel, that Bobi Jones experienced Christian
conversion. The significance of this experience is
reflected not only in his personal development
but also in his writings. In fact, spiritual rebirth,
with all its concomitant aspects, is one of the
major themes of his poetry, and one that should
not be lightly or slightingly overlooked. Rightly
viewed, it is a key to any balanced and empathic
appreciation of the deeper levels of his work.

He had shown a religious interest or inclination
from a young age. There had been an atmosphere of respect towards religion in his childhood home and thus, following his parents'
example, he had attended the family's Baptist
church in Pentyrch Street three times each
Sunday. (His father later moved to Woodville
Road where he was deacon.) When he was six or
seven years old he had expressed a desire to be a
missionary, and that desire remained intact until
his college days. The romance of being a missionary amongst black people in Africa had
appealed to him. Then, during the war, he had

14

expressed a pacifist persuasion. Pacifism was strong in the Minny Street Congregationalist chapel which he had started to attend at the suggestion of Elvet Thomas when he was in the sixth form. But his pacifism went deeper than a mere conformity to his Nonconformist environment. In 1949 he was called to appear before a tribunal to defend his views as a pacifist, and defend them he did (although his father did not agree with his stand) with a bravery and gusto which was to characterize his literary persona in later years. But this social involvement and dedication, admirable though it was in many respects, was, he later felt, all on a humanist rather than a spiritual level. Yet, his religious inclination in this period is further demonstrated by the fact that he accepted the occasional invitation to preach in various chapels near his home.

Those rationalistic arguments of his Marxist grandfather had somehow played their part also in awakening in the young man a longing for the spiritual dimension in life. But probably the greatest landmark on his pre-conversion pilgrimage was his discovery of Saunders Lewis. Under Lewis's influence, from the midst of a secular humanist situation, he had started to consider the encroaching reality of the supernatural. During his year of study at Dublin, he would be seen, every Sunday, at the Catholic Mass. He had also read widely in the literature of various religions, and had started to consider intelligently the claims of orthodoxy. Generally, however, he was not kindly disposed towards the experiential and orthodox Protestant Faith.

And then came the uninvited experience that Sunday evening at Llanidloes. His presence at the only Welsh chapel in the town had been motivated by purely cultural considerations. The sermon was preached and it had no impact. However, before the communion, the preacher read a passage from the gospel of Luke. Reading verse 21 in chapter 22—*But, behold, the hand of him that betrayeth me is with me on the table*—he paused, and Bobi Jones, realizing that until then he had only played in a dilettante manner with religion, knew that he had now been apprehended by God. Confronting Christ as reality, not myth or ideal, he came into contact with the living God. That experience, the commencement of a new and vital relationship with God, and then the development of that relationship in all its deep and wide-ranging implications, is a theme which was to reverberate throughout his artistic endeavours.

After his conversion, he was still drawn for some time to the Church of Rome. During that year in Dublin he was drawn to its emphases upon the supernatural, the miraculous, the need for redemption and the sacraments, and the whole aesthetic and sensuous dimensions to its worship. He followed a correspondence course on the Catholic religion and, according to Geoffrey Thomas, he found the usual protests against the Church of Rome *shrill and angry, not seeing the big themes that Rome proclaimed, and which were absent in Welsh Nonconformist pulpits. I gave him books on Rome, and he read them dutifully and quickly, but they were negative only, none of those kept him from Rome, and he was very near converting for a long time. But the Welshness of*

*Calvinistic Methodism and its founders always earthed him in the protestant orbit (rather like Dr Lloyd-Jones).*

The Welsh language was not thriving in Llanidloes, and so, in 1954, the young teacher accepted a post as head of the Welsh department in the new comprehensive school at Llangefni. His pupils gained excellent examination results, and he was then, as in later years, an efficient and inspiring teacher. He also continued his practice —which was to become a custom—of publishing poems and articles in Welsh periodicals, particularly Y FANER. Between 1954 and 1955, for instance, Y FANER printed a series of articles by him on 'Saunders Lewis y Dramodydd' *(Saunders Lewis the Dramatist)*. In such articles, we see his confident beginnings as a literary critic. But he had not yet published his first book, a significant event for most authors.

That event took place in 1957 with the publication of his first collection of poems, Y GÂN GYNTAF *(The First Song)*. This volume contained poems which contrasted boldly with the mellow muse of the Georgian poets. The opening lines of the first poem (which gave the book its title) is typical of the collection's youthful and confident tone:

*Angau, 'rwyt ti'n fy ofni i*
  *Am fy mod yn ifanc*
*Am fod fy ngwaed yn telori wrth wthio 'ngwythiennau.*
*Cryni yn y fynwent, heb hyder*
*I ddangos i mi dy ddihengyd.*

17

> *(Death, you're afraid of me*
> *Because I'm young*
> *Because my blood warbles as it thrusts my veins.*
> *You quake in the graveyard, lacking confidence*
> *To show me your getaway.)*

The thought expressed here, though not derivative, is analogous to the main thought developed in John Donne's sonnet 'Death be not proud . . .' The poet's first book had an immediate impact and gained for its author an Arts Council award (the first of its kind in Wales); many poets, then and later, have testified to the collection's power and influence.

In 1956 Bobi Jones was appointed lecturer and head of the Welsh department at Trinity College, Carmarthen, a post which he held until 1959 when he was appointed lecturer in education at the University College of Wales, Aberystwyth. This was an important move because he was to remain at the mid-Wales town of Aberystwyth for the next thirty years. By now he was part of a community of Welsh writers: amongst his acquaintances were Waldo Williams, T. Glynne Davies, Pennar Davies and Gwenallt. Bobi Jones, in 1960, was the main impetus for a nucleus of these writers to get together to form YR ACADEMI GYMREIG *(The Welsh Academy)*. He has given an account of the Academy's beginning, and its later development, in the volume DATHLU (edited by R. Gerallt Jones) which was published at the Academy's twenty-fifth anniversary celebrations in 1985. In the early days, the Academy received its share of disparagement; but by now it has made—and is making—a substantial contribution, in both Welsh and English, to our cultural life.

In 1960, Bobi Jones's second collection of poems was published, RHWNG TAF A THAF *(Between Taf and Taf)*, and this volume was also awarded an Arts Council prize. The title refers to the two rivers called Taf, the one flowing through Cardiff, and the other flowing through the rural landscape of Dyfed. They are symbolical of the poet's transition from Anglicized to Welsh-speaking Wales, an opposite movement to the more usual one shown, for instance, in the life of Glyn Jones. Creative work in this period had to be undertaken in the context of an extremely busy academic schedule. Home life was also busy because, by now, Beti had given birth to their two children (Lowri, in 1958, and Rhodri, in 1962). Beti had experienced some difficulty in bearing children, and there had been miscarriages. When their children were born, therefore, their joy knew no limits. This joy—the joy of parenthood and family life—is a prominent theme in Bobi Jones's numerous collections. But it would be a mistake to interpret these poems as being mainly auto-biographical and narrowly domestic. Critical comments by their author, then and later, show that he was keenly aware of the imagistic and symbolical models of modern literature. Such tendencies are never far from the main stream of his own poetry, and, consequently, the poems of celebration of marital love and family life often seem to point to a wider dimension of eulogistic (and even political) significance.

In 1964 the author decided to spend a year of

linguistic study in the University of Quebec. This was an exciting experience for him and his family, and the collection of poems MAN GWYN *(A White Place)* recorded that experience with all its heady enjoyment of hard academic work and relaxation in a new environment of great natural beauty.

The sixties was an important decade for the author, as indeed it was for many other writers in Welsh. The importance of the period is reflected in academic as well as creative work and one significant aspect of the former activity was the author's pioneering contribution to the field of bilingualism. Deeply involved and interested in both the theoretical and practical aspects of bilingualism, he started to develop and implement a strategy, based on careful analysis, for the restoration of the Welsh language. His Welsh for Adults course was developed, and many books were published—practical handbooks for both tutors and students based on sound theory to assist those who were eager and determined to learn Welsh. This is an important aspect of Bobi Jones's contribution to Welsh life, and his deep involvement in the movement for teaching Welsh to adults culminated, as we have seen, in the establishing of CYNGOR Y DYSGWYR (CYD). As in the case of the Welsh Academy, he was the main spring behind the establishing of CYD, and he was the new society's chairman between 1984 and 1987. In a series of articles in Y CYMRO, Y FANER and Y TRAETHODYDD, he explained why a popular Welsh for Adults movement should be considered central to the task of reviving the language. It is too early to forecast yet how successful this movement will be. Increasing numbers of adults are succeeding in mastering the language, and once they have acquired it they often develop a sharp awareness of the Welsh cultural environment and a keen determination to protect it. However, the really successful implementation of Bobi Jones's strategy would involve thousands upon thousands of new speakers—a significant portion of the whole population of Wales—in the context of a popular movement, analogous to the restoration of the Hebrew language in Israel. Whether this will in fact come about in Wales is yet to be seen, but a growing number of thinking and well-informed Welsh-speakers and educationalists are convinced that this, or a similar strategy, is the only real hope for the language's survival.

His interest in language is reflected in the subject of the original study which he undertook for his doctoral thesis, namely 'A study of a child's linguistic development until three years of age in a Welsh home'. This interest in the phenomena and forms of language was allowed to develop as an important strand in the most ambitious areas of the author's literary criticism. In works such as TAFOD Y LLENOR *(The Writer's Tongue)* and SEILIAU BEIRNIADAETH *(The Foundations of Criticism)* we find a fresh approach to criticism, far removed from the usual fare offered in Welsh. In an erudite review, Professor J. E. Caerwyn Williams has described the four volumes of SEILIAU BEIRNIADAETH as *the most important volumes to appear in Welsh on literary criticism since the publication of John Morris-Jones'* CERDD DAFOD. With his belief that the methodology of linguistics can be applied to the study of litera-

ture, Bobi Jones forces us to look at the foundations of literature and to see literature in a new
light.

In 1967, following a visit to Gambia the previous
year, Bobi Jones published his fifth collection of
poetry, YR ŴYL IFORI *(The Ivory Festival)*. By now
he had left the Faculty of Education and had
been appointed to the post of senior lecturer in
Welsh at the University College, Aberystwyth, a
successor to the much respected lecturer and
Christian poet Gwenallt.

Then, in October 1968, he visited Mexico City.
The purpose of the visit was to represent Wales
in the international poetry convention associated
with the Olympic Games. During the visit to
Mexico City, because of the height of the city and
the lack of oxygen and a tendency in the poet's
constitution, he suffered lung collapse, and came
very close to death. Keenly aware of the fact that
he had stood at death's door, during his period
of recovery he wrote the long poem 'Dieithryn
ym Mecsico' *(A Stranger in Mexico)*—arguably one
of his most lasting contributions to Welsh literature; a remarkable 'sequence of poems' in which
the poet meditates on some of life's deepest elements, both profound and simple, serious and
joyous.

After his recovery and return to Wales, he re-
sumed his academic and creative work with his
usual dedication and energy, though perhaps
with a deeper note of urgency. The heady tur-
moil of the sixties was obvious in most university
towns at the time. Those were the days of the

Paris students' revolt which had been influenced by the political philosophy of Herbert Marcuse. Nowhere in Britain was the atmosphere of the period more pronounced than at Aberystwyth which seemed, at the time, to be at the forefront of the radical nationalist movement in Wales. Feelings ran high because of the approaching investiture of the 'Prince of Wales'; the Welsh Language Society was very active; Welsh blood was spilt in the cause of Wales at Abergele. Such matters constitute the necessary backdrop to understand the literature of the period, and when we read stories such as those in DAW'R PASG I BAWB *(Easter Comes to All)* and the poems included in ALLOR WYDN *(Living Altar)*, recalling the social atmosphere and milieu of the period will help us to appreciate the poetry and prose which were, then as always, rooted in time and place and history.

In 1969, Bobi Jones was honoured with the Ellis Griffith Memorial Prize by the Board of Celtic Studies for the best work on Welsh literature, in the form of various articles, published between 1966 and 1969; and then came the seventies—a prolific decade which saw the publication of a wide diversity of books: SIOC O'R GOFOD *(A Shock from the Void)*—Christian essays; TRAED PRYDFERTH *(Beautiful Feet)*—short stories; TAFOD Y LLENOR—structural criticism; GWLAD LLUN *(The Land of Form)*—the seventh collection of poetry; LLÊN CYMRU A CHREFYDD *(Welsh Literature and Religion)*—a Calvinistic critique of Welsh literature and religion.

In 1978 he was promoted to the academic post of

reader in the Welsh department at Aberystwyth, and in 1979 he was awarded a D.Litt. by the University of Wales and then, in 1980, he was appointed Professor of Welsh language and literature at Aberystwyth. The constant flow of both academic and non-academic work from his pen is truly astounding. Most of this awesome industry took place at the desk of his living-room/study in his home, Tandderwen. A careful and systematic scholar, he would dedicate different times of the day (morning, afternoon, evening) to various projects thus ensuring variety. An avid reader and swift writer, he also places strong emphasis on the importance of thinking and meditating.

In 1976, in an interview with J. E. Caerwyn Williams in the important series of literary studies YSGRIFAU BEIRNIADOL (*Critical Essays*), Bobi Jones declared that he was not going to publish another book of creative literature for ten years. Whatever the reasons for this dramatic declaration, one gets the impression that it was not easy for him to remain silent but he kept his vow and ten years later, in 1986, he published the record-breaking longest Welsh poem in the twentieth century, HUNLLEF ARTHUR (20,743 lines). 1987 saw the publication of the large collection of critical essays LLENYDDIAETH GYMRAEG 1902–1936 (*Welsh Literature 1902–1936*). Also in 1987 the SELECTED POEMS appeared, Joseph P. Clancy's splendid English translation of almost half of the total number of poems which had been published in the seven preceding collections. The year 1988 saw the completion of the four-volume pioneering analysis of literary criticism, SEILIAU

BEIRNIADAETH, and in 1989 the Welsh collection CASGLIAD O GERDDI appeared which contains just over half of the total number of poems of the seven volumes together with seventy-seven new poems, under the title EILIADAU, ORIAU, DYDDIAU *(Seconds, Hours, Days)*. In interviews at the time of Bobi Jones's retirement from his university post in 1989, plans were divulged for future publications of works in progress, and one of these appeared the following year, CRIO CHWERTHIN *(Crying Laughter)*, a collection of six stories, the title story being a semi-autobiographical backward glance at the formative years of youth in wartime Cardiff. In BARDDAS 152–153, December/January 1989–90, two other works in progress were mentioned—one in the field of religious literature (on mysticism) and the other in the field of social literature (on nationalism).

# II

It has often been stated that Bobi Jones's first collection of poetry, Y GÂN GYNTAF, is characterized by a youthful zest and daring. These poems impress us still with their uninhibited air of freedom and joyful celebration of life. They are full of the atmosphere of laughter and discovery, their fresh, lively rhythms and newly-minted metaphors and similes re-creating, with jazz-like energy, the poet's new world, the new creation where Blake's dictum seems to ring true: *If the doors of perception were cleansed everything would appear to man as it is, infinite.*

Without smudging this emphasis, it is equally true that here, in the first collection of poems, there is a critical intelligence at work, manifested initially in the selection of poems. Not all the early poems were included in Y GÂN GYNTAF. For instance, 'Nant y Mwynau', a lyric which deliberately parodied Ceiriog's 'Nant y Mynydd', 'I'r Hynafgwyr', a poem reminiscent of W. J. Gruffydd's '1914–1918: Yr ieuainc wrth yr hen', and 'Dylan Thomas', were all rejected, perhaps because the thoughts expressed in them were too direct and shallow. 'Y Bardd Ieuanc i'r Hen Feirdd' *(The Young Poet to the Old Poets)*, which had appeared on the pages of Y FFLAM in August 1949, was probably excluded not because of its adolescent bravado and apparent disrespectful reference to the deity, but because of its slackness of rhythm and thought.

The poems which were included bear evidence that they are far from being mere gushings of a youthful ardour. The sonnet 'Islwyn', for instance, was altered and improved subsequent to its original appearance in Y FFLAM. The changes show that the young poet's critical faculties were at work, choosing a better adjective here, rejecting an archaism there, reforming the closing couplet and so on. Bobi Jones has exercised this deliberate discipline of revising his own work in the preparation of later volumes, including CASGLIAD O GERDDI and the translated collection SELECTED POEMS (the versions quoted in this essay). Such revisions show that the poet's Lawrentian 'spontaneous fullness of being' (to use Leavis's phrase) did not exclude the exercise of a critical intelligence which is one of the hallmarks of modern poetry.

Y GÂN GYNTAF bears many of the characteristics which were to reappear in later volumes. There is, for instance, the deep and intimate interest in people, as shown in the 'portrait' poems—for instance 'Portread o Leian' *(Portrait of a Nun)*, 'Portread o Fam' *(A Mother)*, 'Gyrrwr Trên' *(Engine-Driver)* and 'Ffermwr Rhyddfrydol' *(A Liberal Farmer)*. In such studies, the poet concentrates on the subject as an objective entity, but is not satisfied with outward 'realistic' similitude. Like Cézanne (who is mentioned in one poem) he fashions and moulds the outward reality to re-create the inner semblance, the soul or essence of his subjects. One of his 'methods' is to meditate on the particular and then 'work-in' more general considerations. The result is often similar to impressionism and later developments in art,

27

closer to modernism and its complexities than more traditional realistic portraiture. In 'Gyrrwr Trên', for instance, one of the three poems by Bobi Jones included in THE OXFORD BOOK OF WELSH VERSE (1962)—the other two were 'Cân Ionawr' *(January Song)*, and 'Gwanwyn Nant Dywelan' *(Spring at Nant Dywelan)*—the poem commences with bold brush-strokes, suggesting the polluting industrial world of the engine-driver. In this unlikely setting, as in the Cornish clay pits of Jack Clemo, God is present, and the engine-driver sings his praise in the words of Ehedydd Iâl's famous hymn to Christian redemption. After quoting the last line of the hymn, the poet, avoiding the preachiness of the old preacher-poets, immediately returns to the concrete, sensual reality of the engine-driver's physical presence:

> *Gan gyffwrdd â'r platiau a'r gêr, fel mwyalchen*
> *Yn rhwbio'i haroglau llysieuog ym mhobman,*
> *A'i faw cnawdol ar yr olwynion, ôl ei rym*
> *Gyda miri'r ffwrnais yn dwym ar yr offer.*

> *(Touching the plates and the gear, like a blackbird*
> *Rubbing its herbal scent into every spot,*
> *And his carnal filth on the wheels, his strength's stamp*
> *With the furnace's mirth warm on the instruments.)*

The same warm, human particularity is revealed in the lines which follow. The engine-driver is given a name and a family. The transformed ordinariness of his sanctified labour and family life humanizes a mechanized environment; even the machine is somehow transformed into a sanctuary:

28

*Yn seintwar, canys yma y meddyliai am Dduw orau*

*(A sanctuary, since here he thought of God best)*

The poem develops in such a way as to weave in the 'natural' presence of God into man's world and activity.

*Heddiw'r Nadolig, gwres ei gartref fydd ar ei foch,*
*Chwys ei blant yn lle chwerthin y piston,*
*Eithr wrth draed braisg yr un Duw yr ymgruda*
*Fel pentref tlws yng nghil mynydd.*

*(Christmas today, the warmth of home on his cheek,*
*His children's sweat in place of the piston's laughter,*
*But at the same God's strong feet he'll cradle himself*
*Like a comely village in a mountain niche.)*

This is an unforced emphasis in many of the early and later poems: God is man's primal or pre-lapsarian context, and consequently it is in relation to God that man is most human and real.

'Ffermwr Rhyddfrydol' *(A Liberal Farmer)* is another example of a 'portrait' poem which has developed into a richly textured meditation, firmly rooted in personality, but giving the poet ample opportunity to develop the themes which interest him most. This time his meditation focuses on his experience of hearing, in the farmer's speech, the forgotten echo of his own language:

*Yr oedd mor dew: ond pan lefarai'i gytseiniaid garw*
  *gwyn*
*Teimlais fel alltud ar gyfandir pell*

*Yn clywed drwy farrau eco anghofiedig*
*Iaith ei sgidiau, iaith ei fol, a hiraeth yn fy mygu*
*A thynnu'r diferion gwaelod o bwll fy nghalon.*

*(He was so stout: but when he spoke his pure harsh*
*consonants*
*I felt like an exile on a distant continent*
*Hearing through bars the forgotten echo*
*Of the language of his boots, the language of his belly,*
*and nostalgia choked me*
*And drew the bottom drops from the pit of my heart.)*

The words *yr oedd mor dew (he was so stout)* are repeated three times and such a relaxed and
humorous interjection counterbalances any tendencies towards unreal idealism or solemnity.
There is plenty of humour in Y Gân Gyntaf,
but it is interwoven with a seriousness of purpose
and cogitation which was to be characteristic of
later volumes also. The predominant note, however, is a joyous affirmation of life. And one of
the most prominent aspects of Y Gân Gyntaf
was its rejection of pessimism and despair. It did
not, however, offer a stance of naive optimism.
In 'Cân Ionawr' *(January Song)* the thrush sings in
a gap *Lle nad oes dail (Where there are no leaves).* Here,
as in Jack Clemo, the background to joy is
wintry and bleak. There is nothing in common
between the thrush and the soil below. The
bird is contrasted against the world of man and
nature:

*Heb arlliw o ddyn arno*
*Cyfyd ei big yn goncwest*
*Gerddorol glir,*
*Ac nid oes dim o'i gwmpas*

*O ffresni a glesni gwanwyn*
*Fel nad amhurir ei wyrth*
*Drwy ei chysylltu â'r byd,*
*Mae yn sioc mewn hanes fwy siŵr na mellt,*
*Mwy cwafriog na bwrlwm baban.*

*(With no trace of man upon him*
*He lifts his beak as a clear*
*Melodic conquest,*
*And there is nothing around him*
*Of spring's freshness and greenness*
*So the miracle is untainted*
*By contact with the world,*
*A shock in history surer than lightning,*
*More quavering than a baby's babble.)*

Although the stance is positive and life-affirming, it is not superficial and shrill. The poet, like the thrush, is aware of the menacing darkness but refuses to be dominated by it. Therefore, the poem, like the thrush's song, faces the forces of darkness head-on. The result is hope-generating and life-vindicating:

*Yn arwr bach, y meini mân a deifl*
*At y gwyll, at y gwyll, at y gwyll.*
*Er na welwyd na phlu na phen*
*Gartref heno, bydd pawb a'i clywodd*
*Yn efelychu'r fflach, yn amlhau'r argyfwng.*

*(A little hero, he hurls the small stones*
*At the dark, at the dark, at the dark.*
*Although neither feather nor head was seen*
*At home tonight, all who have heard him*
*Will imitate the flash, multiply the crisis.)*

31

This poem could be compared with Euros Bowen's 'Hyn sy'n Fawl' *(This is Praise)* from the volume CERDDI which was published in the same year as Y GÂN GYNTAF. The last line of Euros Bowen's poem is a deliberate reversal of R. Williams Parry's cry of anguish:

> *Megis y bu o'r dechrau, felly y mae:*
> *Marwolaeth nid yw'n marw.* Hyn *sydd wae.*

> *(As it has been from the beginning, so it is now:*
> *Death does not die.* This *is woe.)*

Not so, wrote Bowen:

> *Bywyd nid ydyw'n marw. Hyn sy'n fawl.*

> *(Life does not die. This is praise.)*

Euros Bowen, like Bobi Jones, initially wrote in the shadow of Williams Parry. A brilliant and very popular poet, Williams Parry's life-outlook was basically tragic. Many of his poems invite us to taste the bitter-sweet fruits of sadness and despair. Such a pondering of life's dark side is, incontrovertibly, one of poetry's functions; and much of the world's lasting poetry (from the Book of Ecclesiastes to R. S. Thomas) does exactly that. It is equally true that poetry has another function also—that of life-affirmation and praise. This tradition, seen for instance in the Psalms of David or in Hopkins's poetry of praise (for example 'The Windhover'), is often intertwined with an awareness of the tragic, and each predominant world-view does not exclude the other. Bobi Jones belongs more to the tradition of praise—a tradition firmly rooted in the Welsh poetic tradition since the days of Taliesin and Aneirin and which grew and developed through the work of the court poets, Dafydd ap Gwilym and Williams Pantycelyn. His work should be read against this background or in this context of praise.

One should not perhaps overstate the case. We come to poetry for many reasons, to taste *various* fruits from the tree of experience and art; and certainly there is a great variety and span in Bobi Jones's poetry which forbids us to over-classify his work in a restricting manner. Nevertheless, no poet is an island, and one should emphasize the obvious but easily overlooked truth that Bobi Jones's work is 'a part of the main' of the Welsh poetic tradition throughout the centuries. He is, of course, thoroughly acquainted with that tradition as his early and later critical studies bear ample witness; and those who appreciate his poetry at the deeper levels find in it the thrilling reverberations of a *living* tradition of praise.

Of all the early poems represented in Y Gân Gyntaf, one of the most significant and representative is 'Gwanwyn Nant Dywelan' *(Spring at Nant Dywelan)*. Nant Dywelan is a stream in Tref Ioan (Johnstown) near Caerfyrddin (Carmarthen). The poem belongs to that two-year period in the poet's life when he and Beti lived in that locality before the birth of their two children. It is a poem full of the actuality of the here and now, pointing to a real stream and a specific season at a particular time and place. It is also an imagistic poem which employs language

33

in a lively but focused manner to record or rather re-create a personal and spiritual experience.

> *Euthum i mewn iddo cyn ei ddeall,*
> *Ei wybod cyn gwybod amdano.*

> *(I entered it before I understood it,*
> *Knew it before I knew about it.)*

The first word of the poem signals a personal perspective but the verb, in the perfect past tense, also suggests a world of real events. The second line refers to the poet's knowledge of the spring —not a superficial knowledge, not merely a knowing *about*. The subjective, almost mystical nature of the experience is suggested by 'smoke', 'light' and 'unblemished lamb'.

In the first stanza, which uses repetition, comparison, rhyme and, most of all, rhythm, the poet has succeeded—within the compass of nine lines—to convey his breath-taking awareness of:

> *Y bywyd ac ansawdd bywyd oedd yn y nant newydd.*

> *(. . . life and liveliness in the new-born brook.)*

The first line of the second stanza gives further confirmation that the poem's sub-text is a meditation on a religious experience:

> *Mae'r flwyddyn wedi cael tröedigaeth.*

> *(The year has known conversion.)*

Significantly, the immediate aftermath of the

year's 'conversion' is 'energy'. Like Hopkins in his sonnet to God's grandeur, the poet is instinctively aware of this all-pervading energy; this awareness is expressed in mystical language:

*Ef yw'r Dirgelwch diderfyn sy'n cysuro bod.*

*(It [or He] is the boundless Mystery that comforts being.)*

Hopkins's awareness of God's grandeur, power and energy is followed by:

*And for all this, nature is never spent;*
*There lives the dearest freshness deep down things.*

Similarly, the Welsh poet sees the 'energy' and 'boundless Mystery' not only in the wide sweep of the world but also in the detailed, minute activity of the toads and the water-vole. Their life and activity and 'tender feet' are contrasted against 'the carcass of winter'.

The contrast between spring's life and winter's death is continued in the next stanza. Unlike a pedestrian paraphrase, however, the actual poem moves rapidly, like a film montage, from one pictorial sequence to the next:

*Aeth y gaeaf at ei dadau.*
*Bu'n llym; bu'n fyw. Ac wele'r rhain:*
*Y byw a goncrodd y byw, ac angau angau*
*Ar y weirglodd fythol hon*
*Sy'n Groes i'r flwyddyn.*
*Daeth y gwanwyn drwy geg y bore*
*A'i dafod yn atseinio'n daer ar betalau'r dwyrain*
*Fel sgidiau milwr yn dyfod adre.*

35

*(Winter has gone to its fathers.*
*It was sharp; alive. And look at them here:*
*Life has triumphed over life, and death death*
*On this everlasting meadow that is*
*A Cross for the year.*
*Spring came through the mouth of the morning*
*Its tongue clamouring hotly on the petals of sunrise*
*Like the boots of a soldier coming home.)*

It is little wonder that Waldo Williams, in a published interview between the two poets, expressed his delight in his friend's *pictorial* gift. (One remembers Bobi Jones's early and later interest in pictorial art.) In lines such as these, one picture follows on the heel of the foregoing one, creating a realistic/abstract montage. Such a rapid succession of images, often found in simile and metaphor, compelling our contemplation of various aspects of reality, often lies at the heart of the poetic act of creation; and 'Gwanwyn Nant Dywelan', like many of Bobi Jones's poems, has the quintessential effect of lasting poetry partly because of this central use of rapidly moving significant images.

This third stanza, continuing the theme of spring's triumph over winter, and life's triumph over death, uses a memorable and unobtrusive metaphor to link the antithesis with the Cross:

*Ar y weirglodd fythol hon*
*Sy'n Groes i'r flwyddyn.*

*(On this everlasting meadow that is*
*A Cross for the year.)*

36

The reference to prayer in the next stanza is
equally sensitive and unobtrusive. Life's religious
element is not syphoned off to a concentrated
area of religious specialization. It is a part of the
whole of life's unity.

The three *Gwelais (I saw)* are reminiscent of the
visionary significance of seeing in early Welsh
poetry, and the third *Gwelais* moves swiftly from
a contemplation of the waterfall (one of the
poet's favourite water images) to an aesthetic and
mystical awareness of life's meaning.

The poem could well have been brought to a
climactic conclusion there, but it is typical of
Bobi Jones that he should want to avoid Waldo
Williams's or Gwenallt's cloak of prophetic gestures. The poem returns from the sublime to the
familiar; and, as always, the poet's sense of fun
is not far from the scene:

> Bydd ystyr yn yr awel bellach, a bod wrth ei phrofi,
> Ac i lawr wrth yr afon y mae tair cenhinen-Pedr
> Felen felen, wedi cloi'r heulwen yn eu calon
> A hen olwg ddireidus arnynt fel merched ysgol
> Mewn cornel wedi cael cyfrinach.

> (Meaning will rest in the breeze now, exist as it's tested.
> And down by the river are three daffodils,
> Golden, golden, enclosing the sunshine in their hearts,
> And the old look of mischief on them like schoolgirls
> In a corner, sharing a secret.)

Like Waldo and Gwenallt, Bobi Jones has medi-
tated on the significance of being: in his work,
such meditation occurs more often in homely

contexts such as this; and, in meditating upon the infinite, he finds infinite opportunities to smile and to laugh. He might have said, with Yeats:

> When such as I cast out remorse
> So great a sweetness flows into the breast
> We must laugh and we must sing,
> We are blest by everything,
> Everything we look upon is blest.

Significantly, the title of the last poem in the first collection of poetry is 'Cerdd Foliant' (A Poem of Praise), emphasizing the fact that this young poet had discovered his empathy with the old Welsh tradition of praise. This emphasis is seen in the second collection also, RHWNG TAF A THAF, which appeared in May 1960. Here too we find 'portraits' of people and places; and once again there is a willingness to develop a variety of forms: vers libre, sonnets, and (for the first time) englynion. There are plenty of similarities between these poems and those in the first collection. But it would not be correct to surmise that there is lack of development between the two volumes. Although the basic world-view remains the same, the stance is not static. The Blakean note of freshness and innocence is still here as the poet ponders the wonder of things, but as he becomes more aware of the themes which interest him most, there is a deeper note of meditation based on experience.

This second volume showed, even more clearly than the first, that Bobi Jones was a poet of many moods and atmospheres. There is a variety, not only of subjects or themes but also of feelings. It would be far from just, therefore, to characterize his work as being one monotonous hymn of praise; there is plenty of variety and, surprisingly perhaps, some of the best poems (like some of the greatest Welsh hymns) express *hiraeth*—a wistful longing. Such nuances of feeling are present, for instance, in 'Yn yr Hwyr' *(In the Evening)*, where the poet remembers his father (who had died in 1956). There is a wistfulness and merging of contrary feelings as the poet becomes aware that, in spite of the finality of his father's going, he sometimes *comes surging back*. Even in death, there is an affection and a kind of bond between father and son:

*Yn yr hwyr wrth y tân mae fy nhad yn llifo'n ôl,*
*Rhai pethau a wnaethom gyda'n gilydd, a finnau'n aml*
*Yn angharedig. Rhithia yno ei gwrteisi ystyriol*
*A dwyn fy nghalon o fewn cysgod ei raeadr syml.*

*Pan chwyddodd y gofod mawr â'i fwlch ef*
*Ni wyddwn yr arhosai ynof er ei fynd mor derfynol*
*Ac y piciai i'm pen fel petai am ymestyn gartref*
*Yn yr hwyr wrth y tân a'i ddafnau'n gwlychu fy*
    *meddwl.*

*Y tu ôl i gefn y byd, yn yr hwyr wrth y tân*
*Crwydra ei gariad i lawr, wele mae'n dychwelyd.*
*Cwymp drwy 'ngwythiennau i droi eu trydan*
*I oleuo 'nghof â'r dyddiau a fu mor hyfryd;*
*A ffrydiaf ynddo draw hyd hwyr rhyw ddiwrnod*
*At aelwyd ailgronni pawb, stôr pob anwylyd.*

*(In the evening by the fire my father comes surging back,*
*Some things we once did together, and I so often*

*Unkind. And then his considerate courtesy takes form*
*And draws my heart beneath his proud and simple wing.*

*When he expanded the vast space with his own gap*
*I did not know he would stay in me, so final was his*
*  going.*
*And would drop by in my head as if he were stretching*
*  at home*
*In the evening by the fire, his feet on the shelf of my*
*  mind.*

*Behind the world's back, in the evening by the fire*
*His love comes wandering down, see, it returns.*
*It drops through my veins to switch their electric on*
*To light my recollection with the days that were so*
*  delightful;*
*And I too walk over to the evening of some day*
*To the hearth of all rebinding, the store of all loved*
*  ones.)*

(J. P. Clancy's translation is based
on an early version.)

There is a subtlety of feeling here which is often
absent from the predictable poems of remem-
brance of the *bardd gwlad*, and it is perhaps significant that Bobi Jones has not followed the
well-trodden path of the *bardd gwlad*, although he
holds great respect for the folk tradition. His
poems, generally, spring from deeper sources
than extrinsic occasions such as birth, marriage
and death. Even his many poems to children
have a significance beyond the immediacy of
parenthood. Whatever the surface theme or subject of a poem may be, beneath the rock face of
the poem, the strata of images and symbols, and
their wealth of meanings, are seldom absent.

In his use of images and symbols, he could be compared, of course, with the French Symbolists —for example Baudelaire, Mallarmé, Rimbaud and (most similar in life-outlook) Paul Claudel. Nearer home, the Welsh poets most similar to him in this respect were Euros Bowen, who wrote a book on the French Symbolists, and Waldo Williams. We cannot but be impressed by the fertility of Bobi Jones's images, symbols and a wide gamut of other poetic devices. Like Dafydd ap Gwilym, he is a master of *dyfalu* (poetic comparison), and also like Dafydd ap Gwilym he is not willing to be held down by the nets of literary conventions and traditions. In other words, as in the work of most true artists and innovators, there is a sense of freedom, a willingness to branch out and experiment. This does not involve a repudiation of the Welsh tradition. That tradition is assimilated and used as a base; and in the best poems the tradition is alternately both present and respected and unreservedly jettisoned in a venturesome spirit of poetic abandon.

This combination of a sense of tradition and a sense of freedom and newness is demonstrated in 'Athro Ysgol' *(School Teacher)*. Perhaps inspired by Elvet Thomas—but also a paean of praise to all gifted schoolteachers—the poem uses many allusions to colourful figures in Welsh history and mythology. The poem is alive with a quickness of touch, an electric movement from allusion to metaphor, image or symbol, all serving to deliver the poet's praise, full of joy and humour, to the schoolteacher—that much abused defender and champion of Welsh culture.

*Arddwr y plant beunyddiol! Filwr cenedl!*
*Mi folaf sialc dy wallt tra bo ynof anadl.*
*Oni chefaist wyn ei boen gan gleddyf Arthur,*
*Gan stranciau Twm Sion Cati cyn gwynfyd Gwener?*

*(Ploughman of the daily children! Soldier of a nation!*
*I will praise the chalk of your hair while I have breath.*
*Haven't you had the pure pain of Arthur's sword,*
*Of the pranks of Twm Siôn Cati, before the bliss of*
   *Friday?)*

The network of feeling in this first stanza develops from open praise, which portrays the schoolteacher as *soldier of a nation*, through realism *(chalk
of your hair)* and a humorous use of history and
myth (Arthur and Twm Sion Cati), finishing in
light-hearted realism *(bliss of Friday)*. The poet
moves his brush swiftly through various nuances
of feelings; and uses the abrupt transferences
from past to present to good effect.

There is much humour in this poem, but veiled
within the humour there is a seriousness of tone.
It is not that the poet is making a point or has
designs upon us; he presents us, rather, with the
complexity and rich tapestry of experience. This
poem, with its references to legends and colourful characters from the Welsh mythos, is reminiscent of Ted Hughes's famous essay MYTH AND
EDUCATION in which he argues in favour of pre-
senting children with legends and myths, not
just utilitarian facts. It also reminds one of Bobi
Jones's later epic poem HUNLLEF ARTHUR *(Arthur's
Nightmare)* which displays a similar interest in the
rich tapestry of Welsh history and myth. The last

two stanzas of 'Athro Ysgol' contain the main thrust of the poem:

*Mae gwlad mewn dyn; a thrwyddi lleda wledydd*
*Fel gwawr yn estyn atynt basiant bysedd.*
*Ti hefyd yw'r afon dros eu clustiau; y rhaeadr a'u*
  *cluda'n*
*Wreichion am haul; tir a dŵr eu hymchwilion.*

*Mae rhith mewn afon; Orphews wyt, a thonni*
*O flaen pob einioes fach, a byrlymu i fyny*
*Tua byd rhydd dynion, a'u harwain o'r tywyll*
*Heb edrych unwaith yn ôl at wag eu ffynhonnell.*

*(A land's in a man; and through it he opens out lands*
*Like dawn reaching a pageant of fingers towards them.*
*You're the river across their ears as well; the waterfall*
  *that carries them,*
*Sparks for a sun; earth and water of their searchings.*

*A wraith's in a river; you are Orpheus, rippling*
*Before each little life, bubbling up*
*Towards a free world of men, leading them from the dark*
*Without once looking back to their empty well-spring.)*

*A land's in a man* . . . The preceding section of the poem culminates in this epigrammatic generalization which then opens out into the very effective allusion to the story of Orpheus leading his wife Euridice out of Hades. The schoolteacher leads the pupils out of the darkness of self and ignorance *towards a free world of men*. Unlike the story of Orpheus and Euridice, there is no turning back. The allusion to the Greek myth, its sad ending transformed, presented in conjunction with the aforegoing allusions to the Welsh myths, adds to the richness of the poem. The pageantry and pantomime of the schoolteacher's perform-ances before the children, unknown to them, was a significant vehicle of emancipation to the free world of adults. The flow of sensibility within the poem shows a sensitive awareness of the psychology of education but, needless to say, it is not an academic treatise: the poet's craft is demonstrated in his use of *proest* (half rhymes) and alliteration, for example, *gwynfyd Gwener*; and *cynghanedd – goledd gwylaidd, basiant bysedd*, as well as the use of metaphors, similes and allusions previously mentioned.

Mentioning the use of *cynghanedd* leads to the fact that Bobi Jones has not chosen, as a rule, to use *cynghanedd* as it is most often used in the tradition —in pre-set forms and metres. It is true that in RHWNG TAF A THAF he presented, for the first time, five *englynion*, but such strict-metre poems are rarely encountered in his work, and only two *englynion* are included in CASGLIAD O GERDDI. He did not 'make a business' of the traditional forms of *cynghanedd*, but this was not from lack of know-ledge or expertise. Anyone who had the privilege of following his pioneering course in creative writing at Aberystwyth will know that he has a deep and practical knowledge of the traditional metres. His decision not to concentrate on the *cynganeddion* in their off-the-peg style was prob-ably a part of his general aesthetics or literary strategy. Like Waldo, he had an aversion to 'filling form'. Recognizing and emphasizing the importance of *cynghanedd* in the Welsh tradition, he preferred to use it as the need arose—like T. Gwynn Jones in his later *vers libre*—rather than as a completely evolved form. In this respect, we can place him in the same 'school' as Alun Llywelyn-Williams who, as R. Gerallt Jones has shown in SEICOLEG CARDOTA, is an important poet—like Bobi Jones from a Cardiff background —who did not follow the more traditional rural school of *cynghanedd*. We should remember, however, that there are many elements of *cynghanedd* in Bobi Jones's poetry, and he has certainly not reacted or polarized against its judicious use; in his critical studies (particularly TAFOD Y LLENOR and SEILIAU BEIRNIADAETH) there are many perceptive references to *cynghanedd*.

One of the most personal and autobiographical poems in RHWNG TAF A THAF is the *vers libre* poem of place, 'Caerdydd' *(Cardiff)*. The capital city of Wales is an important locale in Bobi Jones's poetry, and his attitude towards it is ambivalent. 'Caerdydd' is a poem which helps us to understand the poet's attitude not only towards the capital but also towards the Welsh language. It is true that some of his poems, for example 'Merch Siop' *(Shop Girl)*, as Alan Llwyd rightly indicates in his BARDDONIAETH Y CHWEDEGAU, show the corrupt influence of the town and city as juxtaposed against the simpler, more authentic rural life. But it is not a simple matter of preferring the country life and condemning the city. Cardiff retains the poet's respect. Indeed, he has said that

*although I have lived most of my life outside Cardiff, I remain a city poet. Cardiff, the 'capital city' of Wales, that paradoxical theme, is the essence of much of my poetry, even when I am writing about the winter in Quebec. It has followed me everywhere.*

45

The poem 'Caerdydd' reveals an attitude both critical and respectful towards the city. The opening brings to mind Eliot's vision of the unreal city in 'The Waste Land'.

*Yma lle y treia Taf ei math o fôr undyn*
*Rhwng muriau gwythïen na châr y gwaedlif du*
*Mae blas anobaith, pontydd traffig i bob-man*
*Heb gyrraedd yr un, a'r holl orffennol gwlyb*
*Heb berthyn i'r dyfodol. Yma y treia Taf.*

*(Here where the Taf ebbs its sort of one-man sea*
*Between the walls of a vein with no love of the black*
*    haemorrhage*
*There is a taste of despair, bridges of traffic to every*
*    where*
*Not reaching any, and all the wet past*
*Not belonging to the future. Here the Taf ebbs.)*

The poem, then, seems to divert on a tangent, not describing Cardiff at all, but reverting to the poet's acquisition of the Welsh language.

*A minnau'n llanc agored i ysbrydoedd*
*Fe ddarfu iaith i mi fel digwydd byd.*

*(And I, as a lad open to spirits,*
*Language happened to me as a world occurs.)*

The suggestion made in the apparent digression is that the future of Cardiff as a real capital city is inextricably bound up with the future of the language. There is an honest attempt to evoke the exhilarating joy of acquiring the language. This is often the testimony of many who have succeeded in learning Welsh; the experience has

46

opened their eyes and hearts to a new world at their doorstep. Bobi Jones has often attempted to give form to this feeling, almost like a conversion, of discovering the language, or rather being discovered, being moulded anew, by it; the language giving his life a new direction, a new dimension and significance.

> Llywiodd fi
> Rhag strydoedd dur, drwy goridorau clercod
> Budr eu cenfigen a'u hunan-falchder brics
> Ar hyd papurau punt a chwantau neis
> At fae. O sut dywedyd cic fy llygaid
> O weld y gwahaniaeth rhwng yr hyn a fûm
> A'r cyfle i fod yn grwn fel nas breuddwydiwn?

> (It guided me
> From hard streets, through corridors of clerks,
> Foul their envy and their self-conceit of bricks,
> Along pound notes and nice lusts
> To a bay. Oh how to tell of the kick of my eyes
> On seeing the difference between what I was
> And the chance to be whole as I had not dreamed
>     of being?)

But there is also present in 'Caerdydd' a realistic awareness of the plight of the language, and the linguistic/national crisis is embodied, as in an 'objective correlative', in the desolate no-man's land of the city.

> Yma lle y treia Taf ei math o fôr undyn
> Mae'r dŵr yn cilio, yn troelli'n chwydrel sur
> Ac yn ferbwll. A fydd yma beth yn unman bellach?
> Ai crai wastadedd cras? Ai dail crych
> Heb ddyfnder glas? . . .

47

*(Here where the Taf ebbs its sort of one-man sea*
*The water retreats, swirling, sour sludge*
*And a stagnant pool. Will there be anything further*
*   anywhere here?*
*A raw dry plain? Crumpled leaves*
*Without blue depth? ...)*

There is a genuine questioning, the concession of a real possibility of defeat. But the poem does not end there. The poet's optimistic realism leads him back to allowing a possibility of hope —hope for the language, for Cardiff and for Wales:

*Os felly, llawenhawn*
*Am y dŵr sydd yma ar ôl; ac na chynilwn.*
*Iechyd da, pob hwyl, i Dduw a fu'n ymsymud*
*Ar wyneb dyfroedd. Iechyd da i'r Iachawdwr, i'r Un*
*A godai ddyfroedd bywiol o bydew cenedl.*

*(If so, let us rejoice*
*For the water that is left here; and not hoard.*
*Cheers, good luck, to God who has been moving*
*On the face of the waters. Cheers to Him*
*Who would raise living waters from a nation's well.)*

The biblical allusion in the last line—Christ's words to the Samaritan woman in John 4:10— indicates that even though the condition of Wales is indeed desperate, with 'the gift of God' things would be different. Here again is demonstrated the poet's basically optimistic stance: he is existentially aware of the negative factors which militate against the language's survival and therefore, to a large extent, the survival of the Welsh identity; but he steadfastly refuses to buckle under to the temptation to submit to cynicism and despair. In Wales, as in other cultures in crisis, there is yet ground for hope. There is One who could again raise out of the nation's dark well *living waters* both spiritual and cultural.

We now go on to the third collection of poetry, Tyred Allan *(Come Forth)*. This collection was published in May 1965. By this time, Bobi Jones was in his prime, a 35-year-old lecturer in education at Aberystwyth, father of two children (Lowri was seven and Rhodri three) and a very busy writer of academic studies, prose and poetry.

The general response to his poetry so far had been mixed. He had come third in the Crown competition at the National Eisteddfod of 1950. His *nom de plume* was *Nisien*. Two years later, at the National Eisteddfod in Aberystwyth, one of the adjudicators for the Crown competition was Professor W. J. Gruffydd, the romantic Georgian poet and influential member of the old guard. Bobi Jones had expressed his view, in the *Pabell Lên* (the literary tent) at the Eisteddfod in Caerffili, that Gruffydd was more of a literary figure than a significant writer. Later, Gruffydd in 1952 thought one of the competitors *(Efnisien)* was Bobi Jones. In fact, *Efnisien* was Harri Gwynn and Gruffydd later inadvertently admitted to Harri Gwynn that his *pryddest* 'Y Creadur' *(The Creature)* had not won the Crown because he had mistaken it for the work of Bobi Jones.

It is not an overstatement to say that there was a kind of literary and academic vendetta against Bobi Jones in some quarters. The godfathers

rarely committed their attacks to print, but it is
their influence one senses in punishing reviews
such as D. H. Culpitt's of Y GÂN GYNTAF (in
Y TYST) where the disparaging claim is made
*Os bu bardd cocos erioed dyma enghraifft ohono (If there was*
*ever a bardd cocos* [a rhymester] *here is an example of*
*one.)* There were others who responded to his
work in a more balanced manner. One of these
was Gwilym R. Jones. T. Llew Jones and Euros
Bowen had also responded favourably to RHWNG
TAF A THAF and—most important of all—the
68-year-old Saunders Lewis, in an interview with
Aneirin Talfan Davies in 1961, had referred
favourably to his work.

In 1962, at the National Eisteddfod in Llanelli,
Bobi Jones had won the first prize in a competition which asked for a collection of poems. It
was this collection which formed the nucleus of
TYRED ALLAN published three years later. This
volume was a watershed. It contains themes and
styles that were present in the first two volumes,
but here the poet seems to home in more frequently on his main themes; there is a sharper
focus, a surer touch—the disciplined mastery
of a poet who is firmly based in a confident
knowledge of his vision and literary resources.
Saunders Lewis said of this volume (in a review
in the WESTERN MAIL):

*bardd y mae ganddo beth o arglwyddiaeth Shakespeare ar*
*iaith yw Mr Bobi Jones. Y mae sbonc greadigol mewn*
*pennill ar ôl pennill o'i lyfr newydd, a bygythiad gweledigaeth*
*bron iawn ym mhob llinell. Dyma'i lyfr gorau ef: y mae ei*
*afael ar arddodiaid ac ar idiom yr iaith bellach yn gadarn*
*ddiogel. Pan dyr ef reol yn awr, fe'i tyr o fwriad chwarae;*

*y mae ei eirfa yn ddihysbydd ysgolheigaidd ac yn gyfoes fyw . . . yn y gyfrol hon y mae cyfnod aeddfedrwydd bardd y mae dydd i ddydd yn traethu ymadrodd wrtho yn agor, ac y mae ynddi addewid am bethau gwych iawn i ddyfod.*

*(Mr Bobi Jones is a poet who has some of Shakespeare's mastery of language. There is creative bounce in verse after verse of his new book, and the threat of vision in almost every line. This is his best book: his grip on the language's preposi- tions and idiom is by now safely firm. When he breaks a rule now, he breaks it with playful intention: his vocabulary is inexhaustibly scholarly, alive and contemporary . . . this volume contains the commencing mature period of a poet for whom day unto day uttereth speech, and there is here promise of great things to come.)*

In Casgliad o Gerddi (1989), significantly more poems are included from Tyred Allan than from all the other previously published collections. Such a fact is interesting because Bobi Jones is a perceptive critic, and the insight we gain from watching his selective procedure in relation to his own poetry is, perhaps, more significant than is usually the case. In this context it is interesting to know that his two favourite poems before Hunllef Arthur (*Arthur's Nightmare*) were the re- vised version of 'Adroddiad Answyddogol o'r Drefedigaeth Olaf' (*Unofficial Report from the Last Colony*) and the revised version of 'Gwlad Llun' (*Land of Form*). His favourite poem from Y Gân Gyntaf is 'Rhiannon'.

In a published interview in Barddas, he divulged what seem to him to be the major themes in his poems:

*One of the major themes—if not the most major of them all
—is rejuvenation, resurrection, or regeneration. A theme
which is completely contrary to the fashionable major themes
of the twentieth century.*
(BARDDAS 147–8, July/August 1989, 8)

The first poem in TYRED ALLAN sets the key.
'Bwyta'n Te' *(Having Our Tea)* could be compared
to a painting by one of the Dutch masters. It is a
study of a homely family scene. The atmosphere
is quiet and relaxed, the pace steady: nothing
demonstrative here, no dramatic, eye-catching
gestures. And yet, in the unruffled family scene,
the poet senses a Presence, both powerful and
benign, who seems to have arranged the meal.

*Mae 'na rywbeth crefyddol yn y modd yr eisteddwn
Wrth y ford de, yn deulu cryno o dri.*

*(There's something religious in the way we sit
At the tea table, a tidy family of three.)*

The tone is conversational, almost prosaic. But
it is a controlled tone, a deliberate probe to the
edge of poetry. The theme of 'Bwyta'n Te' is the
sacramental nature of even the lowly, 'ordinary'
act of a small family sharing a meal. This is a
recurring theme in Bobi Jones's work, explored
in numerous poems. It has also received his
attention in critical studies, for example in his
excellent 'Sagrafennaeth a Llenyddiaeth' *(Sacramentalism and Literature)*—a chapter in YSGRIFAU
DIWINYDDOL 2 *(Theological Essays 2)*, 1988, where,
mentioning Paul Claudel, he touches upon some
of the similarities between sacramentalism and
symbolism.

*. . . every visible thing is an expression of God's grace, and consequently a meeting place between God's powers and man's need. And this is also true from one aspect—is it not? —that every single thing we see, every tree, every mountain, every house, is greater than the thing itself, and speaks to us of its deeper world and meaning.*

This is a strong, controlling vision throughout Bobi Jones's poetry. In an ordinary person or place or situation, he often senses an extra-ordinary presence which reminds us of the presence in Wordsworth's 'Prelude'. In Y GÂN GYNTAF, the presence is usually felt in the world of nature, sometimes with an almost pantheistic subjectivism. Later, as the poet matured doc-trinally, he was more aware of the pantheistic 'danger', but continued to sense and perceive, within an orthodox Christian framework, the immanent presence of God in all that was about him—especially in the context of the family. As the *tŷ* (house) was a central symbol for Waldo Williams, so the *teulu* (family) is a central symbol for Bobi Jones. In a period of our history which has seen an onslaught on the concept of family, it is surely significant that this Christian poet has given it prime of place at the centre of his artistic endeavours.

The poems about children should be seen against this background; symbolically they are closely connected to the central theme of rebirth and resurrection. In many of the poems to children we can hear the sounds of laughter, which is in sharp contrast to the sounds of anguish we hear in much modern literature. The sonnet 'Gweddi Plentyn' *(A Child's Prayer)* is in the *soned laes* form

53

(where the length of the lines varies beyond ten syllables). As in Hopkins's sonnets, there is ample use of alliteration which sometimes develops into *cynghanedd*. There is much use of contrast and paradox in this sonnet: God is contrasted with *Brenin Braw (King of Terror, death)* and then with the little girl; she is then contrasted with dealers in violence, and then heaven's angels. The joy of her prayer is contrasted with the pain of prayer in the world. Further, the central paradox of the poem is similar to the paradox of the incarnation. Out of the mouth of babes God has ordained strength.

'Gweddi Plentyn' is a very successful poem. The references to God are innovative without being unseemly or over the top. For instance, *fe ddaliwn Dduw (we hold God)* is fresh and appropriate. In some of his younger references to God, the poet had left himself open to the just charge of lacking taste. In his maturity, we see him searching for new modes of expression, fleeing clichés, without falling into the trap of impropriety. Even in his maturity, there are occasional examples of bad taste, not in references to God but, once or twice, to mortal loved ones. For instance, 'Corfflosgi Mam-gu (ar fy mhen-blwydd)' *(Grandmother's Cremation [on my birthday])* makes one feel slightly uneasy. Could it be that the poet, here, failed to achieve enough artistic distance to take sufficient heed of the pitfalls inherent in such a theme?

'Gweddw' is a much more effective poem. This is an impressive example of Bobi Jones's ability to empathize deeply with another person and to give his readers an insight into another person's predicament. No comfort is offered. Indeed, by studying the widow and portraying the anguish of her loss, there is a deliberate avoiding of the superficial clichés of sympathy. What comfort others offer has a hollow ring:

> a phob orig fach yn dyfod
> Yn dragwyddol, meddent. Mwyach, fe'u gwariwyd oll.

> (and each short hour became
> Eternal, they'd say. Now, they've all been spent.)

These last words of the poem, although negative and comfortless, through the power of 'negative capability' help us to meditate on life's true riches—not material possessions but those unrepeatable moments of shared blessings. A similar effect is produced in 'Trempyn'. The poem enters into the world of the tramp, piling image upon image to depict his strange, unmaterialistic lifestyle. His wealth is his closeness to the earth. Like the widow whose minutes with her husband have all been 'spent', the tramp has also spent his leaves. The true wealth is in the fellowship which can exist between one human being and another, in personality, and in kinship with the natural environment.

'Hen Wreigan' (Little Old Woman) belongs to the same category of poems. As in 'Gweddw', the poet addresses the subject of his poem in the second person. At first, this has a humorous effect because such words would not ordinarily be spoken in the context of everyday discourse:

*Madam, fe fu'r gwyfyn yn eich gwallt.*

*(Madam, the moth has been in your hair.)*

As the poem proceeds, however, the use of the second person helps us to see the little old woman in close-up. Her shipwrecked appearance at present is juxtaposed against her beauty a mere fifteen years ago. The poem hinges on this juxtaposition; the final effect is one of tragic wonder at the irony of ageing.

Some of Bobi Jones's best poems—in the early and later period—show his concern about ageing and death. These poems demonstrate his realistic awareness of this aspect of the human condition. Such an awareness could degenerate into cynicism and despair, but these extremes (often present in modern literature) are avoided because of the poet's Christian instinct to affirm life's value and worth even in the face of death. The awareness of death seems to deepen the poet's appreciation of life; life and love are more real to him because he cannot ignore the presence of the spectre at the feast.

The title TYRED ALLAN *(Come Forth)* appears as a phrase in one of the sonnets in the collection, 'Aderyn y To' *(Sparrow)*. They are, of course, Christ's words to Lazarus. The bird sings in a most unlikely place—on the roof of a tax office! Even in such a desolate place, without trees and without the greenery of his natural habitat, the bird sings. This sparrow, therefore, reminds one of the thrush in 'Cân Ionawr'. His song is compared to Christ's voice which, through *the con-*

*fidence of Mary and Martha*—through faith—can give life to the dead. The sparrow, like the poet, is a singer of praise and similar to *the Voice which has been a Cauldron of Rebirth*. Here the allusion is to the magical cauldron in 'Branwen Ferch Llŷr', the second branch of the MABINOGI. The bird's song, Christ's voice, the poet's song, the cauldron of rebirth all belong to that cluster of potent images which help define Bobi Jones's central themes.

Jeremy Hooker has claimed in THE POETRY OF PLACE: *Some Welsh poets of European stature have in this century continued to write from place, from deep within a communal experience, with a poet's confidence equal to Wordsworth's. Waldo Williams is a modern instance of the visionary poet in a sustained and sustaining relationship with a living tradition, who wrote from a countryside which was also the ground of his culture.* This sense of place, an almost primitive awareness, is present also in some of Bobi Jones's many poems to places. It is found, for instance, in 'Afon Cleddau' *(River Cleddau)* and 'Y Mynydd Du' *(The Black Mountain)*. In both of these poems there is a 'pagan' acknowledgement of the unique, personalized quality of a particular river and a particular mountain. The river has a reviving, almost healing effect on the poet's spirit before he returns to the world of people. Like a painting of an unspoiled Welsh landscape, the river of the poem, with all its dance and joy, is an image not easily forgotten.

*Ac yna ennyd yn ystod*

*Fy nisgyn, yma ar ymyl y lan, ryw hanner llath*
  *Oddi wrth y dŵr, fe ddistawodd fy holl feddwl.*
*Gwasgarodd y cwbl fel gwair: collais grap ar bob math*

*O gredo ac o ffeithiau. A'm hynni yn anial*
*Fe'i gwelais—y llawenydd oll ohoni, ei thro*
*Wrth chwerthin, ei ffordd o fyw, gyda'i bwrlwm gwamal*

*Iach.*

> *(And then for a moment, while I was*

*Descending, here on the edge of the bank, half a yard*
*From the water, my whole mind fell silent.*
*Everything scattered like hay: I lost my grip on every sort*

*Of credo and of facts. And with my life-force a wasteland*
*I saw her—all the joy of her, her bent*
*For laughing, her way of living, with her frivolous wholesome*

*Bubbling.)*

The craft of the poem should not go unnoticed. There is use of internal rhyme, alliteration and *cynghanedd*—the latter, once more, an unobtrusive part of the whole—*y llawenydd oll ohoni; a gwyllt yw ei chalon dan y gelltydd.* A *terza rima* scheme is used with *proest* (a kind of half rhyme or linkage), each stanza, before the final couplet, employing accented and unaccented rhymes alternately. The broken lines at the end of one stanza running over (*goferu* which means *enjambment*) to the beginning of the next suggests the uneven but continuous dancing flow of the river.

In 'Y Mynydd Du', the mood is more Wordsworthian, hushed and reverential. Again there is that paganism which we first encountered in 'Y Gân Gyntaf':

> *'does fawr*
> *Y gellid ei wneud â'r mynydd hwn ond crymu 'lawr*
> *I'w addoli.*

> *(there's not much*
> *One can do with this mountain but bow down*
> *To worship it.)*

This is no glib, picture-postcard empathy with nature. There is a genuine respect, an appropriate fear.

> *Nid rhyfedd i emynwyr dynnu eu bwyd a'u llyn*
> *Yn amlach na'r gwartheg yn y parthau hyn . . .*
> *Mae'r mynydd yn fy nghadw i mewn dychryn.*

> *(No wonder hymnists drew their food and drink*
> *More abundantly than cattle in these parts . . .*
> *The mountain keeps me in terror.)*

A harbinger of the modern 'green' consciousness, this attitude towards nature is at opposite poles to the materialistic, exploitative attitude which has been so prominent in our society since the Industrial Revolution. It is the otherness of the Black Mountain that lingers in our memory. Nature has an autonomy from the world of man, and is to be respected for her own sake, not merely for utilitarian, man-based reasons.

Bobi Jones's awareness of place is such that many of his poems of place—like an artist's impressions on canvas—capture some of the unique characteristics of various locations. Nevertheless, it would be a mistake to consider the various places as merely extraneous grist for the poet's mill: they have more inner symbolic significance than locations in a travel guide. In 'Afon Cleddau' and 'Y Mynydd Du', for instance, there is an element of surprise and wonder—the poet did not choose these locations as 'subjects' in a cold and detached manner. As the last poem in TYRED ALLAN reminds us, he believes in the *awen (poetic muse)*; thus, in his poems of place, as in his poems to people, there is usually a 'given' quality.

Between October 1963 and May 1964, Bobi Jones (and his family), by arrangement with Laval University, spent a year in Quebec. This was supposed to be the first in a series of such visits to various bilingual countries which he hoped to make every five years or so as staff-member of the Education Faculty at Aberystwyth.

The *awen* followed him to Quebec and forty-six of the poems he wrote during his stay in Canada were included in MAN GWYN: CANEUON QUEBEC (1965). In his short preface to the collection he acknowledged his debt to Alun Talfan Davies who had encouraged him to publish this book so soon (about six months) after the previous collection. (Most of Bobi Jones's books have been published by Llyfrau'r Dryw/Christopher Davies press which was owned by Alun Talfan Davies.)

Primarily a year of academic study, the stay in Quebec turned out to be a highly creative period for the poet. A note about the contents of MAN GWYN on the dust-jacket explains that although the book contains many of the author's simplest poems, he did not remember composing most of them. The adjective *gwyn* in the title, as Joseph Clancy explains in the notes to the SELECTED POEMS, *carries strong meanings of 'blessed' in Welsh as well as 'white', and 'a white/blessed place' has the proverbial meaning of another one better than where one is—in English terms, that other side of the fence where the grass is always greener.*

It is not difficult for a Welsh person, particularly a writer in the Welsh language, to see the *man gwyn* of other developed nations where writers are not burdened with the problems and complexities which face the Welsh writer. This is the a priori of such poems as 'Hiraeth' *(Homesickness)* and 'Porthladd Quebec' *(Quebec Harbour)* where the attractions of Canada are juxtaposed against the disadvantages of Wales. Despite its disadvantages—its inferior political status, and psychological complexes regarding identity—the poet, paradoxically, opts for Wales. Although the immediate locale of the poems in MAN GWYN is Quebec, there are many backward glances eastwards. The poet does not idealize his own country, he refuses to pretend that all is well and that the manifest corruptions do not exist; yet, as poet and thinker, it is to Wales that he gives his allegiance. This is his country, his microcosm, and despite all its imperfections, his attitude towards Wales is, ultimately, positive rather than negative. This is one reason for his perseverance as a writer: unlike many of the muted voices of defeat, he has not allowed the negative factors, so abundant in Wales, to defeat his instinctive will to write.

The political strand is hardly ever completely

absent from his poetry. In the Introduction to the SELECTED POEMS, the translator, Joseph Clancy, quotes him as follows:

*... I have a feeling that more of the poems are political than some readers consider—even most of the 'love poems'—and certainly the 'family poems' ... living in Wales itself, it is rather difficult to deal with Spring or water or people or places without being desperately political. To use a Welsh word is still a revolutionary action. Even to exist is just a little bit of a social attack.*

Clancy rightly emphasizes that *Nationalism is not, however, a separable element in Bobi Jones' work—any more than are the other central experiences separable elements: love of the natural world, of wife, of children, of neighbour, of nation, of God through Christ, these are experienced as a unity within single poems as in the total body of work.*

Perhaps there is sometimes a danger, in concentrating on a particular locale, be that at home or abroad, for the poet to lose some of that generality of experience to which we expect poetry, somehow or other, to aspire. In some of the best poems in MAN GWYN, the poet rises above the geographical and more directly political themes. 'I Beti' *(To Beti)* and 'Na Choelia'r Cusanau' *(Do Not Believe These Kisses)*, for example, despite their highly personal theme of marital love, succeed in conveying a general human experience in a particular context. Incidentally, the latter of these two poems contains an excellent example of *gair mwys* (ambiguity)—one of Bobi Jones's favourite poetic devices reminiscent of the metaphysical poets—inevitably lost in translation. The loved one is addressed as *fy noeth* where *noeth* can be read as *naked* or as *wise one* (the mutated form of *doeth*).

Poetic generality is also achieved in 'Lleuad Olaf yr Ugeinfed Ganrif' *(The Last Moon of the Twentieth Century)* which was written in 1964 when moon-landings were being planned but had not yet been accomplished. This poem, with its long lines, a series of eight couplets ending in un-accented rhymes, is more successful than some of the poems in *traethodl* form (for example, 'Traethodl y Gwynt a'r Gân' *(The Wind and the Song)* which can easily deteriorate into a mono-tonous watered-down *cywydd*.

'Atgyfodiad yr Adar' *(The Resurrection of the Birds)* is one of the successful *traethodl* poems. There is here an effective use of repetition, occasional *cynghanedd* and alliteration, metaphors and similes. The colourful use of personification reminds one of Dafydd ap Gwilym, but the poem rises above a mere echo of the past master through its subtle references to modern society; for example,

> *Mae ffrwydrad eu poblogaeth*
> *Yn broblem. I glercod caeth*
> *A llywodraeth y weirddol*
> *Mae eu gweld nhw'n llifo'n ôl*
> *Fel hunllef i'w trefn wastad,*
> *I undod gwynundon eu gwlad.*
>
> *(Population explosion's*
> *A problem. To captive clerks*
> *And the grassland government*
> *Seeing them flooding back is*

*A nightmare to neat order,*
*Their land's white-toned unity.)*

The birds have developed into a symbol of that life-affirming *variety* which is an important element in Bobi Jones's political and aesthetic outlook.

*Yn lle'r un oer—amlder cariad:*
*Adar sy'n aradr i'r wlad.*

*(For cold's sameness—love's bounty:*
*Birds are a plough to the land.)*

The importance of the particular which has general significance is nowhere better demonstrated than in 'Chwech y Bore' *(Six in the Morning)* —one of the most resonant *vers libre* poems in Man Gwyn. On the surface it is a study of awakening after a sleepless or restless night. (The poet's tendency towards insomnia is reflected in numerous poems and stories.) The night is equated to death's tomb and the morning, as it quietly unfolds, to life. Here, as in early poems, there is a mystical awareness of the life-affirming essence of things:

*cariad y bywyd sy tu mewn i bopeth*

*(the love of life that's within everything)*

Firmly rooted in the particular, the poem occasionally branches out into the general, sometimes by the use of one word, for example 'the new day's *tradition*', 'the *eternal* morning'. There is also a sacramental significance to this awakening:

> *cododd adar y to ar eu penliniau,*
> *ac i wyll daear dyn*
> *cawod o golomennod fel litanïau*

> *(sparrows rose on their knees,*
> *and into the gloom of man's earth*
> *a shower of doves like litanies)*

The last line in the poem, balancing with its beginning like shadowed perspective in a painting, highlights the theme of death (with suggestions of the last supper) in the midst of life:

> *ac eto*
> *fel pe bai aroglau angau o hyd ar doriad bore'r*
> *bwrdd*
> *yng nghalon fy nghanu mae beddrod.*

> *(and yet*
> *as though smells of death were still on daybreak's*
> *table,*
> *in the heart of my singing there's a tomb.)*

Most of the poems in the fifth collection, YR WŶL IFORI *(The Ivory Festival)*, were occasioned by the poet's visit to Gambia in 1966. 'Dawns y Du' *(The Dance of the Black)* is a long poem in four parts which uses different voices. It is the first of the long poems which are precursors to HUNLLEF ARTHUR *(Arthur's Nightmare)*. Discussing the latter, Bobi Jones has explained that in a long poem he does not attempt to achieve a uniform lyrical intensity throughout the poem. Parts of 'Dawns y Du' are rather monotonous but one of its most impressive sections is *Python* which is read by the poet on his long-playing record where he explains the background to the poem. It is based on an incident in which the poet, unexpectedly countering a python in the bush, proceeded to kill it with a stick. The description of the snake and the poet's feelings of self-forgetting hatred demonstrate a brilliant dexterity of expression. As in D. H. Lawrence's 'Snake', the depiction of the outward scene is matched by a forthright psychological self-analysis. The moment of high excitement—killing the snake—leads to a remorseful self-knowledge at the end. As in many other successful poems, metaphors depicting life are juxtaposed against metaphors depicting death. This is an area of experience and awareness which inspires the poet to the zenith of his art.

This is also one of the dominant characteristics of the most memorable poems in ALLOR WYDN *(Living Altar)* (1971), rightly considered by many to be Bobi Jones's best collection of poetry. The life/death juxtaposition is found in 'Dieithryn ym Mecsico' *(A Stranger in Mexico)*, surely one of Bobi Jones's most outstanding accomplishments, a 'sequence of poems' which stands unique and unsurpassed amongst the greatest Welsh poems of the twentieth century. The background to the work is explained at its commencement: the sequence deals with a visit the poet made in October of the Olympic year 1968 to Mexico City as the representative from Wales for the International Cultural Olympics. As it turned out, the Mexican government prevented the poets from meeting because of the political threat which they posed! All the same, the visit could hardly have been more traumatic for the Welshman:

*During that visit, because of the city's altitude and the scarcity of oxygen together with a special bent in the poet's temperament he was on the brink of death. His life was saved by a young woman who was working at the hotel Del Paseo, namely Purificacion Calvillo. This sequence of poems is a meditation fashioned later on in the weakness of his sick-bed.*

There are fifteen sections to the sequence. The first section is in four stanzas, each stanza containing three lines which rhyme, similar to early gnomic poems such as those found in the ninth- to tenth-century Llywarch Hen cycle:

> *Y deilen honn, neus kenniret gwynt.*
> *Gwae hi o'e thynghet!*
> *Hi hen; eleni y ganet.*

> *(This leaf, the wind carries it away:*
> *Ah, sorry its lot.*
> *It is old; it was born this year.)*

There is a deliberate echo of this poem in the second verse:

> *Awyren lwyd ym mwgwd wybren,*
> *Beth ydyw hi? Hi hen.*
> *Crina yn Hydref absen.*

> *(Grey plane in a mask of sky,*
> *What is it? It is old.*
> *It withers like October absence.)*

By such means we are presented with concrete pictures of real events which also convey in a highly disciplined mode the artist's meditation on life and death. It should be noted that dif-

ferent poetic forms are employed throughout
the sequence thus ensuring variety. There is also
unity of thought and meditation as the poet
develops his theme from section to section.

The central part of the sequence is the fifth
which depicts the poet facing death. Such is the
remarkable intensity of this section that it helps
us to realize that death is one necessary and
important aspect of Bobi Jones's main theme of
resurrection. If such a comment seems too
obvious, it should be remembered that elsewhere
—in his most pioneering works of criticism—
Bobi Jones has drawn our attention to the simple,
basic contrasts (sound/silence, presence/absence,
etc.) which exist, he claims, at the heart of language and literature. Such a basic contrast (life/
death) is certainly found throughout 'Dieithryn
ym Mecsico', and its fifth section is the convincing, artistic testimony of one who has returned
from the brink of death.

Such a theme could get out of control and
deteriorate into melodrama, sentimentality or
moping self-pity. But, although the first person
is used (watchfully), there is a Shakespearean
objectivity and almost mocking clarity as man,
proud man, is shown face to face with the sleep
that rounds his little life.

The parallel use of humour and seriousness is
very effective, but there is a deliberate avoiding
of what Professor Clancy has identified as *the
modernist safety-net of irony*:

*Nid oedd dim eironi*

*Mwy yn y diwedd, nid oedd dim amwysedd na dim amheuon.*
*I'r ffaith y deuthum. Y digwyddiad cras. Yr hanes.*

*(There was no more*
*Irony at last, no ambiguity, no doubts.*
*I entered the fact. The crude event. History.)*

Although irony, as dominant posture, is rejected, there is—in this section and throughout the sequence—an unstrained attendance to the multi-layered nature of the crisis. The simplicity of the situation is perceived and acknowledged; so also are its various layers and aspects. In other words, there is both concentration and depth of meditation.

Following the hymn-like praise of the sixth section which expresses the poet's faith in Providence, the seventh section is a close-up of Purificacion Calvillo, the young woman who saved his life. A letter from Bobi Jones to Geoffrey Thomas and his wife Iola—written in Mexico soon after the crisis—helps us to appreciate this section of the poem, and also helps us to appreciate the significance and importance of this experience in Bobi Jones's life. Here a part of the letter is translated from the original Welsh:

*The saving of my life was completely 'unreasonable' according to the world's standards ... I was staying in a hotel where there was one receptionist (who works part-time) who had had exceptionally good training as a nurse in California, although no-one else there knew anything about this background. She had had excellent experience with heart complaints. There 'happened' to be an oxygen cylinder in the hotel. It was completely impossible for a doctor to arrive in time. But she took control of things, and she was shouting commands to the hotel manager as if he were a servant. She pulled me out of the beast's claws by a hair's breadth . . . The Lord Jesus's goodness towards me, and his unmerited love towards me throughout these last days is too glorious ever to put into words . . .*

The eighth section, following the experience of God's kindness and providential care, is a song of praise full of appreciation even of life's difficult aspects. Here a Calvinistic joyful appreciation of God's presence in all corners of life and experience reveals a bedrock certainty which is far more convincing than a superficial cognitive cloak or attitude. The joyful celebration of God's reality and loving care is comparable to that found in great Christian poetry throughout the ages.

The ninth section is a moving account of the sick poet awaiting his wife's arrival. She had been informed of his illness and was flying out at once to be by his bedside. Friends and relatives in Wales were, naturally, greatly concerned at the news of Bobi Jones's illness but Geoffrey Thomas, giving comfort and support to Beti, was given an unusual degree of certainty that all would be well. In the ninth section, the praise to Beti—no unusual development for this poet!—has a new depth and power based as it is in the real life paradox of weakness and mortality. The tenth section offers a restrained meditation on the significance of love face to face with death.

A prayer of humble confession and new dedication is followed by a childlike chant of joy (based on the Mexican 'festival of the dead'). In the thirteenth section, there is a change of mood as the poet meditates on his approaching return to Wales. This meditation on the positive values represented by Wales—community, variety, etc. —develops, unobtrusively, into prayer on behalf of the country's spiritual and material welfare.

The fourteenth and fifteenth sections depict the poet's return to his home country. After the joyful return is celebrated, the sequence ends with a new dedication and prayer to be better prepared for death.

Although 'Dieithryn ym Mecsico' can be taken to represent a supreme moment in Bobi Jones's art, there are other poems in ALLOR WYDN which are a significant accomplishment. The fifth section of 'Adroddiad Answyddogol o'r Drefedigaeth Olaf' *(Unofficial Report from the Last Colony)* is an honest analysis of the poet's relationship with the Welsh language; writing in Welsh is a kind of compulsion, and the sixth section reveals the reason: behind the outwardly harmless mien of the language there is a volatile power and potential for change.

Love towards his language and country was present in Bobi Jones's muse from the beginning; however in ALLOR WYDN the patriotic theme is given a new prominence and of all Bobi Jones's collections, this one shows most clearly the influence of the Welsh political and linguistic tensions of the 1960s and early 1970s. Such factors doubtlessly explain in part the effectiveness and power of such poems as 'Capel Celyn'. This poem

71

(like 'Gweddw' on another theme) does not offer any comfort. It merely presents and analyses the tragedy of the mindless destruction of the Welsh language and culture as represented by the drowned village.

*Y peth na allent ei ddeall, hynny a ddistrywiasant,*
*Y peth hen hwnnw, mor uchel a lluniedig.*

*(The thing they could not comprehend, that they have*
  *destroyed,*
*That ancient thing, so lofty and finely wrought.)*

The poem is a brilliant, restrained, but razor-sharp representation of the national calamity facing Wales—the destruction of its way of life by the government purporting to represent it. This theme is explored in other earlier and later poems. In such poems as 'Gwlad Llun' (*Land of Form*), the cultural calamity is viewed, not only in the context of misgovernment, but also in that of Welsh moral decline and corruption issuing from its spiritual infidelity.

This theme becomes increasingly prominent in the Gwlad Llun collection (1976) which is included in the Welsh Casgliad o Gerddi but only partly represented in the English Selected Poems. The awareness of death was present from the beginning (Y Gân Gyntaf). In the later poems, it is increasingly seen not only as a personal threat but as a general all-pervading pollution threatening the entire environment. The theme, however, is most powerful in its personal context. 'Pan Rodiwn' (*When We Stroll*), a poem of five stanzas, is a meditation on the inevitable separation of death that awaits all married couples. Joyfully aware of his wife's presence when they stroll together, the poet dreads the day they will have to be separated by the final enemy. As in all Bobi Jones's best poems there is here a strong controlled passion where the immediate focus of meditation is not diluted by extraneous considerations. Not attempting to express too much at once, the poet is content to allow the poem to develop and reach fruition on its own terms. This comparatively short poem, like the 'Dieithryn ym Mecsico' sequence, can be ranked amongst his most significant achievements as a poet. Indeed they may even be considered by some readers to be 'great'—an adjective which is always contestable in the relatively subjective world of poetry.

In 1986, after a ten-year abstinence from publishing poetry, Bobi Jones released HUNLLEF ARTHUR (Arthur's Nightmare), an epic poem (although he called it an anti-epic) of 20,743 lines. From his early student days he had been interested in Arthurian legend but the scope of HUNLLEF ARTHUR is wider than its Arthurian theme, wider also than the various events and colourful persona from the Welsh past which appear in it.

The poem is divided into twenty-four parts. The first part presents that perennial figure of Welsh nationhood, Arthur, sleeping in a cave. The 'nightmare' of the poem, as in a surrealist film, is a montage developed around this central motif. We are then presented with different historical periods, usually connected with particular persons, such as Llywelyn, Dafydd ap Gwilym, Owain Glyndŵr, Charles Edwards, Lloyd George. Because of its wide sweep, its daring raids on all periods in Welsh history, the poem seems to offer a description or perhaps more accurately a symbol of the Welsh nation. As in Gwenallt's work, Wales is both rebuked and praised, hated and loved. The last section, *Datguddiad*, ends with the cryptic words: *mi enir rhywbeth (something will be born)* contrasting with the poem's opening *Bu farw breuddwyd (A dream died)*.

The poem was inspired by its author's mature knowledge of the Welsh psyche (one remembers his interest in psychology from an educational perspective)—his knowledge of the *fear* that often characterizes the Welsh, their lack of confidence (because of the colonial experience) concerning their own identity and status in the world. The poem should be read, as Professor R. Geraint Gruffydd has explained, against the background of the Renaissance idea of epic poetry. The Homeric ideal in nineteenth-century Wales did not produce much lasting poetry and against such a background, as Geraint Gruffydd says, one admires Bobi Jones's bravery for tackling this *massive and unfashionable task*.

He was well-endowed for the task by his keen awareness of the tradition of long poems through the centuries: Homer, Lucretius, Virgil, Dante, Luis de Camoes, Milton, Lönnrot, Wordsworth ('The Prelude') and Kazantzakis ('Odyssey', 1938). He had also read 'The Bridge' by Hart Crane and 'Canto General' by Pablo Neruda, although he had not liked the former and had not enjoyed parts of the latter. Perhaps Charles Williams's 'Taliessin through Logres' should also be mentioned. In any case, it would be foolish to look for direct 'influences' because poets of stature assimilate 'influences' and make them their own, but his knowledge of other long poems in other languages and periods of history probably helped to give him the confidence he needed to feel that his task was worthwhile.

One of the dangers which threatens the reader's enjoyment of any long poem is monotony, and HUNLLEF ARTHUR, despite its innovative use of 'blank verse', has not completely escaped this danger. J. E. Caerwyn Williams (one of the poet's former colleagues at Aberystwyth) has also drawn our attention to the over-intellectual parts of the poem. *On the other hand,* Professor Williams added, *there are exquisite sections, quite as good as the poet's best short poems, and these appear so often that reading the poem is as pleasant an experience as sailing down one of the world's great rivers.* Geraint Gruffydd drew our attention to the often repeated line

*Tu hwnt i amau y mae dinas wen*

*(Beyond doubt there is a white [or blessed] city)*

This, he explains, is Saint Augustine's City of God. Professor Gruffydd adds:

*. . . there is here much more than a series of symbolic characters presented dramatically and arranged (roughly) in chronological order. The complete work is given unity by the author's vision of his nation's history as a product of the clash between the will of the Welsh themselves—often a deficient*

75

*will—and God's intervening grace. In other words, the vision is thoroughly Christian, Augustinian in essence and Calvinist in its details . . . the poem deserves hard study, the sort of study devoted to the world's great epic poems as they were gradually acknowledged as classics.*

Dewi Stephen Jones went as far as to claim *This, for me, is the best long poem in our literature. Certainly, it is one of twentieth-century Europe's literary masterpieces.* Not all reviews were so kind but most of the poem's readers would agree with J. E. Caerwyn Williams that the best way to approach the text is to be alert to what Bobi Jones has termed *canolbwyntiau tyndra (centres of tension)* or *boglynnau uchafbwyntiol (climactic clusters)*. Sometimes these appear in the form of personal or even 'autobiographical' material such as the elegy to the poet's mother in the nineteenth section, 'Creu'r Proletariad' *(Creating the Proletariat)*. Such personal material is always assimilated into the historical and mythical themes. For those who, like one reviewer, protest at the merging of history and myth, one answer is that Bobi Jones is in the good company of Shakespeare in this respect. It will take time for us to judge properly the status of HUNLLEF ARTHUR in the body of Welsh literature. All of its reviewers seemed to be aware that HUNLLEF ARTHUR is a significant work of literature. Perhaps its central significance is the fact that it offers us a poetic mirror of myth in which we may catch the fleeting reflection of our corporate identity as a people.

Some of the central themes of HUNLLEF ARTHUR are found in the eighth section of CASGLIAD O GERDDI (1989)—'Eiliadau, Oriau, Dyddiau'

*(Seconds, Hours, Days)* which is not included in
SELECTED POEMS (1987). The title suggests a keen,
almost obsessive awareness of time passing. Many
of the poems deal with death, but not in a mor-
bid and negative manner. The work commences
with a poem called 'Rhagair i Fawl' *(Preface to
Praise)* which stresses the importance of having a
positive rather than a negative outlook. One
remembers Clancy's reference to the modernists'
*safety-net of irony*. The later poetry of praise continues to show Bobi Jones's rejection of irony as
a constant underflow or sub-text. Rejecting the
unthinking cynical attitude, he shows, with
characteristic sophistication and intellectual
toughness, that another basic attitude and set of
presuppositions are available to the modern
writer. It is this basically positive stance that lies
behind some of the apparently negative passages
in the later poetry. Nevertheless, we find chilling
references in 'Eiliadau, Oriau, Dyddiau' to an
end-of-humanism era where holocausts, mass
abortions, the Chernobyl disaster and nuclear
despair are the norm. In this bleak landscape, the
poet continues to express a hope which is rooted
in Christian realism. One of the best poems here
is 'Mynd am Wyliau' *(Going on Holidays)*, a meditation on the Christ-centred hope of the resurrection as contemplated from a husband-and-wife
perspective. There are also hymn-like poems of
praise, together with more multi-layered poems
of meditation on themes such as the complex
cultural situation in Wales and the life-enriching
results of language revival.

> *Estroniaid fyddwn ni nes trown ein gilydd*
> *Yn bobol wahanol.*

*(We will be foreigners until we turn each other
Into a different people.)*

In Bobi Jones's poetry, even when the mood is
sombre, there is hope and intimations of joy and,
in Saunders Lewis's words in his commendation
of RHWNG TAF A THAF,—*bygythiad gw`eledigaeth (the
threat of vision).*

# III

From his earliest writing onwards, Bobi Jones has written creative prose as well as poetry. Indeed throughout his career as an author he has taken a keen, practising, interest in the writing of novels and, in particular, short stories. It should be emphasized that this interest in prose-writing was more than a corollary to the writing of poetry. It was something that Bobi Jones, with his usual blend of mischief and moral earnestness, took seriously.

His first novel, published in 1958 and following hard on the heels of his first collection of poems, was NID YW DŴR YN PLYGU *(Water Does Not Bend)*. The protagonist is a student of medicine by the name of Siôn Preece. His friend, David Jones, is also preparing for the same profession. Their school of medicine is located in a large town called Grandfield. Siôn is uncertain about his calling and he finds his superficial relationship with a girl named Rhiannon unhelpful. His relationship with his parents (his father is a minister) is also problematic. The main part of the novel is located in David's home village, Llanlecwydd. There Siôn falls in love with David's sister Mary who is disabled and restricted to a wheelchair. David's family and the other inhabitants of Llanlecwydd are told that their valley will be flooded to provide water for Grandfield. (Flooding Welsh valleys for English convenience was a dominant issue when the novel was writ-

ten: Tryweryn was destroyed in the early sixties.)
Rhiannon finds that she is expecting Siôn's baby
but he refuses to marry her, and consequently
Siôn's father, who lives in London, disappointed
with his son, commits suicide by drowning. The
novel ends with Siôn's awareness of the negation
and failure that has characterized his life so far.

The main theme of the novel, according to the
author's comments twenty years later in an essay
under the title 'Tua'r Eldorado?' (*Towards the
Eldorado?*) in FY NGHYMRU I (*My Wales*), was the
inadequacy of optimistic and romantic nationalism when faced with the absurdity and inner
corruption (*syrffed, llygredd mewnol*) of existence.
The novel's main interest lies not in its surface
realism but in its Lawrentian probing into psychological states and motivations. There are dream-
like sequences similar to those which reappear in
later short stories. Another interesting element
in the novel is the light it shines on places and
themes in its author's life and poetry, for example Nant Dywelan, the stream used as the
central image and part of the title of one of his
best poems in Y GÂN GYNTAF (discussed earlier),
appears here also.

The other early (less successful) novel, published
in 1960, BOD YN WRAIG (*Being a Wife*) again, according to its author, deals with romantic nationalism. But, unlike the first novel, there is an effort
to confine the feelings of negation within one
character—the man, and the romantic ideals
within another—the female. But the fate of
romantic nationalism is the same in spite of the
superficial success. Significantly the author, in

parenthesis, uses the word *allegory* when referring to the two novels. Their thrust, he explained, is found in their titles: darkness without repentance in NID YW DŴR YN PLYGU and the effort to submit lovingly in BOD YN WRAIG. In his interview with J. E. Caerwyn Williams in YSGRIFAU BEIRNIADOL IX, he admitted that he considered both novels, generally, to be unsuccessful personal experiments in his struggle with the problem of the story. Perhaps the key words here are *struggle* and *problem*; in spite of the effective parts, there is a certain lack of artistic integration and wholeness, and we do not find that sense of ease and dexterity which is usually present in accomplished prose, even when such prose is deliberately self-conscious and experimental. There are also, at times, in both novels, signs of too much haste.

In 1966, Bobi Jones published his first collection of short stories, Y DYN NA DDAETH ADREF *(The Man Who Did Not Come Home)*. There is a clear contrast between the prose in the best of these stories and that of the two novels. First of all, the author seems to have taken greater care with his sentences. There is a clearer focus, a steadiness of touch and that impression of effortless ease, already mentioned, which is usually found in accomplished writers of prose, however diverse their objectives and styles may be. The story which gives the collection its title is a light-hearted account of a successful tale of love. Beneath the surface level of the story there is a subtle meditation on providential positive irony of circumstance. In the third story, a vivid cameo depicting an eighteenth-century interlude

which is ruined by an itinerant preacher, the
author is dealing with another main-line theme
—the unnecessary conflict between pietism and
culture. In 'Y Gêm' *(The Game)* we find the vivid
but unreal atmosphere of a dream. Perhaps the
American in this story is a personification of
futile modern bureaucracy with its technocratic
lack of vision but, although Bobi Jones has referred to it as the best story in his first collection,
and although it contains effective Kafkaesque
elements that were to reappear in later stories,
'The Game' seems to me to be impaired by a lack
of appropriate focus. Generally, however, the
stories in this collection show that Bobi Jones
was able to use the form of the short story in a
confident and sophisticated manner.

His second collection of short stories was Cı
Wrth y Drws *(A Dog at the Door)*. The title story is
a first-person account by an artist who regularly
visits Scotland to work in solitude. During one
of these visits, a mentally-handicapped neighbour comes to his door. In a compassionate
account of his persecuted life we are told that he
is completely dependent on his mother, but in
his hand he is carrying her suicide note. Her plan
had been for them both to make their exit together but he broke free to his new captivity
without her. The author's aphoristic gift is
demonstrated in such maxims as *nid oes gwyliau
rhag yr hunan (there is no holiday from self)*. In 'Bad
Achub' *(Lifeboat)* and 'Y Tŷ' *(The House)* there is a
strong element of symbolism. In the latter—
which is related in the present tense—a wife who
lives in Labrador and aware that her husband and
two sons are in mortal danger (they are out at

sea and lost in a storm) burns her house to use it as a beacon to guide them home to safety. Through his restrained use of such symbols, the author's strong poetic imagination allows new nuances of feeling and significance to emerge without undue emphasis on the symbolical substructure. 'I Indiaid yn Unig' *(For Indians Only)* is a narrative in the form of a diary based on the author's experience in Quebec in 1964. There are some revealing passages which affirm the impression created by the poems of MAN GWYN—that the Canadian experience helped the author to define his cultural and intellectual position. For instance, he mentions Gustave Guillaume, the French linguist whose systematic, structuralist and dynamic theory of language was developed by Bobi Jones in the context of literature.

In the third collection of short stories, DAW'R PASG I BAWB *(Easter Comes to Everybody)* (1969), the first story, 'Diwedd y Byd' *(The End of the World)*, is a story about a flood with apocalyptic overtones. 'Tu Hwnt i'r Gors' *(Beyond the Marsh)* is a successful main-line story. It relates a reporter's attempt to interview an author in his rural surroundings in the region of Cardigan's Cors Caron. This author's son wears the uniform of the 'Free Wales Army' (much in the news during the period before the 1969 investiture at Caernarfon). The father is very evasive and wears an expression of suffering and guilt. In the end, the young man in uniform reveals that he, the son, is the secret author of his father's work. In this story, unlike 'Y Gêm', we are presented with a situation which is both realistic and symbolical which seems to be open to meaningful interpretation.

83

We are not left to flounder in mystification; neither is the 'meaning' of the tale given on a plate. There is a satisfactory artistic balance between revelation and concealment.

In the penultimate story in this collection of seven, there is a focused use of the surrealist element in the personification of death. Here, as in many of his stories, the author's main theme seems to be his central character's destiny face to face with death. Death is an important theme in the poetry, as we have seen, but there the approach and context is usually more life-affirming and eulogistic. In his prose, the author often seems more concerned to pose problems, to place his characters in difficult hypothetical situations to see what the outcome will be. He is not satisfied with raw realism. The approach is similar to that of the scientist who presents a hypothesis or the philosopher who poses a moral problem. Reading these stories, we are aware that the author, like Kafka (who is named in the fifth story) or Jorge Luis Borges, is creating an imagined world in order to deal with moral and spiritual matters which are hinted at but not defined. These moral and spiritual considerations are not, of course, crudely emphasized. We are in the world of fiction, not theology. But nevertheless they are there, in the background, providing a certain parabolic ambience and atmosphere, which can be both challenging and deliberately disconcerting.

The last story, which has the same title as the book, deals with the Easter Rising of 1916 in Ireland. It relates the story of Patrick Pearse, shot by the British, and the story is rooted in historical reality. It is an early example of Bobi Jones venturing into the field of historical fiction and it is a creditable attempt, which succeeds in drawing our empathic response. Here again, death plays a leading role, and the meditation on patriotism and sacrifice was not a remote and hypothetical matter in the Wales of 1969. The Welsh blood which was spilt during the highly politicized investiture was commemorated in two poems. As Joseph Clancy explains in his note on 'Cost Arwisgo 1969' *(The Cost of an Investiture 1969), Bobi Jones, who had tutored Prince Charles in an intensive course in Welsh language, literature, and history at Aberystwyth before the investiture, also wrote a poem for the two 'First Martyrs of the Nationalist Movement', to which he appended a note stating that while he profoundly disagreed with 'the military means of defending our country', he could not join in 'the flood of easy and merciless condemnation of two who —whatever is said of their methods—loved Wales unto death'.*

TRAED PRYDFERTH *(Beautiful Feet)* (1973), the fourth collection of short stories, contains a variety of realistic and dream-world stories. The book's title is taken from the longest story in the collection, again a piece of historical fiction, which relates the story of David Jones (1797–1841), the Welsh missionary to Madagascar. Like other leading members of the great Welsh missionary movement in the eighteenth and nineteenth centuries in various parts of the world, he made a significant contribution to Madagascar's history and, although his wife and child died and were buried at Tamatave, he resolutely succeeded, with David Griffiths's assistance, in translating

the Bible into Malagasy. It is interesting that Bobi
Jones should have chosen him as subject for his
story because—as was mentioned earlier—as a
young boy of six or seven he had heard a missionary giving an address in a chapel and, until
his college days, it had been his ambition to go
as a missionary to Africa. The first part of the
story is set in the form of David Jones's imaginary
diary. The second part is in the form of a 'play'
(in ten scenes)—a relatively new departure for
Bobi Jones (although he had won a competition
for writing a radio play in the Dolgellau Eisteddfod of 1949, and has taken a keen critical interest
in the form).

Many of his critical writings show that Bobi
Jones has a lively and well-informed interest in
history. His wide reading in history is also evident
in HUNLLEF ARTHUR. The 'Traed Prydferth'
story and later works of historical fiction were
well received, but interestingly—in the interview with J. E. Caerwyn Williams—it is other
stories in the collection which are mentioned by
Bobi Jones as being main-line stories: 'Dowch i
Ddawnsio' *(Come and Dance)*, 'Pobl mewn Oed'
*(Grown Up People)*, 'Gast' *(Bitch)*, 'Cusanau Ffarwél'
*(Farewell Kisses)*, 'Daffodiliau i Charlie' *(Daffodils for
Charlie)*. In these stories there is an almost night-
marish atmosphere. They—perhaps more than
the early historical pieces and the more realistic
stories based on direct experience, such as 'Y Ffos
Olaf' *(The Last Ditch)* which was translated for
TWENTY-FIVE WELSH SHORT STORIES (Oxford University Press, 1971) – show the distinctive nature
of Bobi Jones's contribution to Welsh prose. As in
the work of his South American contemporary

Gabriel García Márquez, there is a poetic element of 'magic realism' in many of his most significant stories.

Many distinguished writers of short stories—Chekhov and Maupassant, for instance—have chosen to develop the form in a realistic tradition. This is certainly true in Wales where authors like Kate Roberts have been more at ease in the realistic mode. However, as Bobi Jones indicates in his chapter on the short story in LLENYDDIAETH GYMRAEG 1902–1936 (*Welsh Literature 1902–1936*), there are other traditions and possibilities. As would be expected of the general editor of most volumes in the significant STORÏAU TRAMOR *(Foreign Stories)* series, he is very much aware of the various possibilities of the short story. His poetry shows his predilection towards experimentation (at least in the sense that he is not willing to cling to yesterday's static forms without venturing to develop them) and this is true of his attitude towards prose-writing also.

'Cusanau Ffarwél', in form and content, shows this interest in experimentation. The story is told in the second person plural *chi* used as singular (creating an ambivalent sense of directness and distance). The narrator addresses the protagonist directly, but the exact context of communication is not revealed. In a later story, 'Cymro ar Wasgar' *(A Welshman from Abroad)*, the intimate second person *ti* is employed. The effect is striking and, because of the unusual and ambiguous point of view, a deliberate sense of unease is created. The story portrays a Welshman on holidays in Brittany. During the outgoing and homecoming journey, and in Brittany itself, he is followed by a mysterious stranger. Even at the end of the story, we do not know the identity of this stranger. In a bizarre development, during the various stages of his appearances, he is depicted as having lost an arm, then a leg, and so on. In the end we are not left with any certainty as to the corporeal reality of this character. Is he a member of the 'secret police' (a familiar figure for many committed Welsh patriots) or is he a phantom from the collective unconscious, a Kafkaesque embodiment of persecution and guilt? We do not know and are not given any neat answers, but the story leaves its imprint on the memory like an expressionist painting, highly atmospheric and open to various interpretations.

We cannot read such a story without being aware of the wavering energy and vitality in this prose which is so different from the smooth sentences of most accomplished Welsh prose-writers. Even in the sentence structures, there is a deliberate, rather self-conscious jerkiness. Such a style may not be conducive to suspension of disbelief: it is more conducive to a Brechtian approach with its deliberate attitude of 'alienation' or 'A-effect'. Bobi Jones has been criticized by some reviewers for the unusual nature of his prose. But we should not jump too hastily to the conclusion that this is the style of someone who has come to Welsh as a second language. Easy though it is to be aware of the unusual nature of the style, we should not overlook its considerable vitality and strength.

In 'Tawelwch os Gwelwch yn Dda' *(Silence Please)*

we find ourselves again in a bizarre but real world where the killing of babies (only a slight extension of the mass-abortion principle) is the norm. Below the surface events of the story, there is a wealth of moral and religious cogitation, partly revealed through the symbolical situation and partly through the narrative and dialogue; for instance, one of the characters says: *The law is no more than what is already natural.* In 'Gast', as in the poem 'Gweddw', we are given a compassionate glimpse, without easy comfort, of a widow's loss and shattered world; and the same compassion arising from contemplation of life's cruel irony is found in the Second World War story, 'Daffodiliau i Charlie', another psychological narrative which takes us, like many others by this author, to a region outside Wales and outside the usual realistic limits of many Welsh writers.

In his prose, Bobi Jones seems to be *exploring that area in story, character and style which lies between the comfortably naturalistic and the anti-naturalistic.* So it is claimed on the back-cover of the fifth collection of short stories which was published in 1977 under the intriguing title PWY LADDODD MISS WALES? *(Who Killed Miss Wales?).* There are ten stories in the collection; most of them are short in length (under ten pages) but two are long (over fifty pages). The title story is one of these and it is one of Bobi Jones's most successful works of prose fiction.

The Miss Wales of the title is the beautiful Gwen who has married a minister of religion named Wyn who holds a watered-down and modernist belief. Gwen has seen the lie at the heart of his life, and their marriage, before the story's beginning, is in a precarious state. Unable to respect her husband or his emasculated beliefs, she turns for comfort to the whisky bottle and to the arms of the adulterous Arthur.

When Gwen's body is found, the cause of her death appears to be suicide, but Arthur—knowing the background—becomes suspicious. Did Wyn kill her? Or was her competitive rival, Miss England, responsible for her death? Finally, by means of Gwen's suicide note, which he had not seen previously, Arthur realizes that it was he, because of his flippant and superficial response to her declaration of love, who was mainly responsible for her self-inflicted death. At the end of the story, not showing any signs of repentance or remorse, he is already eyeing another man's wife.

Within this framework, Bobi Jones succeeds in creating a credible, contemporary Welsh milieu. The dismal but convincing backdrop to his scenario is a valley community which exists, without much vitality or joy, at the end of the mining era. There are passages which bring to mind those atmospheric descriptions with which D. H. Lawrence suggested the warm-blooded industrial community of his novels and stories. There is also a Lawrentian analysis of expectations and tensions within marriage. The main focus of the story, however, is Bobi Jones's rigorous diagnosis of a contemporary Wales which is sick at heart because of its spiritual adultery and moral decline. The dialogue, as in

other stories, is sometimes strained: most characters speak a deliberately standard Welsh; but
throughout the narrative—and even in those
occasional passages where the dialogue is flawed
—the moral analysis rings true.

The mood in 'Y Gwyliwr Nos' *(The Night Watch-
man)* is preternatural and disquieting. Here, as in
many of the other stories, there is a painful,
almost Orwellian, awareness of the vast dangers
posed by a bureaucratic, over-centralized state
system as represented by the despised clerk or
state official. Such a system, with its 'get on your
bike' mentality, does not invest enough faith in
the value of regional diversity. The result may be
more devastating than is at present realized. Bobi
Jones, within the fullness of his art, in both his
poetry and prose, shows the humanizing value
of what Professor Walford Davies (in a published
lecture on Gerard Manley Hopkins) has aptly
called 'devolution of the mind'.

In his *Translator's Introduction* to the SELECTED
POEMS, Joseph Clancy quotes Bobi Jones's opinion
about his poems:

*To use a Welsh word is still a revolutionary action. Even to
exist is just a little bit of a social attack.*

This is true also of the stories. The surrealist element is partly, though not wholly, explained by
the social, political and psychological conditions
which pertain in everyday Wales. For instance,
the unjust conditions of the *mewnlifiad* (the influx
of population into Wales) with its swift corrod-
ing effect on both language and community is

reflected in 'Bro Chwithig' *(Awkward Region)* where the land itself seems to be groaning and suffering from the psychological illnesses of its inhabitants.

Artistic distance in such stories is often achieved by the dream-world techniques of keeping certain elements in the story at a remove from contemporary 'reality'. Another artistic device by which the necessary distance can be achieved is, of course, the programming of a temporal perspective by means of historical fiction: 'Traed Prydferth' and 'Daw'r Pasg i Bawb' are two stories, already mentioned, which are clear examples of such a *genre* and approach. Bobi Jones used the historical option also in 'Merch y Sgweier' *(The Squire's Daughter)*, 'Gwaed Gwyn' *(White Blood)* and 'Canlyn y Wraig' *(Courting the Wife)*, all of which appeared (between 1986 and 1988) in BARN—the monthly literary magazine which (since its launch in 1962) has been an important vehicle for Bobi Jones's prose-writings, particularly in the field of literary criticism. 'Merch y Sgweier' and 'Gwaed Gwyn' were later included in CRIO CHWERTHIN *(Crying Laughter)* (1990)—a collection of six long stories or novellas.

'Merch y Sgweier' takes us back to the eighteenth-century world of the Welsh author Theophilus Evans, Marmaduke Gwynne and his daughter Sara, Charles Wesley's wife. In this mature, meditative work—which could be compared with Saunders Lewis's classic MERCH GWERN HYWEL— we see the clash between the old values (as represented by Theophilus Evans) and the revolutionary old/new values highlighted by the Methodist Revival. The story deals with a theme which has often appeared in Bobi Jones's criticism, namely the apparent conflict between nature and grace and their ultimate harmony and resolution. With an inside knowledge of the reality of grace, Bobi Jones has often alerted us to the real dangers of an unbalanced pietism, and in 'Merch y Sgweier' he presents this rich theme with lyrical finesse. 'Gwaed Gwyn' relates the story of Rhisiart Gwyn, the Catholic poet and martyr. The central theme revolves around the author's meditation on the nature of true religion and the dangers of a misdirected, simplistic, zeal. In 'Merch y Sgweier', he applauds the warm Christianity of the enthusiastic young Methodists. In 'Gwaed Gwyn' he decries the cold brand of Protestant zeal which, in the name of head-knowledge, uses the barbaric methods of the Spanish inquisition, forgetting the centrality of Christian love.

In these recent works of historical fiction, we find a more mature and self-critical use of prose than in the early novels. 'Y Bradwr Da' *(The Good Traitor)*, also included in CRIO CHWERTHIN, is given the subtitle 'Stori am wlad bell' *(a story about a distant country)* and its background is a country under the shadow of Nazism towards the end of the Second World War. Two of the stories in CRIO CHWERTHIN are given a modern Welsh setting, but one of the most arresting contributions to the collection is the title story. Unusually for Bobi Jones's prose writings, this story is semi-autobiographical and it gives us a fascinating glimpse, through the words of the first person fictitious narrator, of the author's childhood and adolescent experiences in Cardiff. The best stories in CRIO CHWERTHIN vindicate the author's interest in the long story or novella, and we may yet see important developments in this direction.

# IV

The startling variety of Bobi Jones's *œuvre* stems, partly, from his inquisitive interest in the multiform possibilities of the genres at his disposal. This fascination with the polymorphic nature of literature is nowhere better demonstrated than in his literary criticism. Throughout his career as a writer he has amassed a body of criticism which is unique both in scope and perspective. The early influence and inspiration, without doubt, was Saunders Lewis. In 1951, after returning to Cardiff from Dublin to study for his teaching certificate, he heard that Saunders Lewis had begun lecturing in the Welsh department and he obtained his permission to attend the lectures. He was captivated by Saunders Lewis's intellectual wizardry: *Memories of those lectures which I used to attend are very sweet to me by now* (BARDDAS, September 1989).

Nevertheless, Bobi Jones's gifts as a critic were apparent before he had met Saunders Lewis in the flesh. A humorous article written by him for his school's magazine YMLAEN in the summer of 1945 (when he was sixteen years old) under the title 'Great Poetry' shows his promising early ability to discuss literature with zest and originality. No sooner had he learned Welsh than he commenced publishing criticism as well as poetry. For instance, in Y LLENOR in 1950 he published a lively study of Emrys ap Iwan's style. Even as early as this we perceive that Bobi Jones,

like most significant critics, held clear views as to
what constitutes great literature. He does not
baulk at introducing moral considerations into
the discussion, and, like F. R. Leavis or T. S.
Eliot, even when discussing style, there is a moral
edge to his writing. This moral awareness was
balanced by an inquisitive and catholic interest
in a wide variety of literary topics, and in his
early articles for Y FANER in the 1950s he wrote
on subjects as diverse as understanding modern
poetry, tradition and creation, the form of the
sonnet and *englyn*, Eifion Wyn, Siôn Cent and of
course—inevitably—Saunders Lewis (a series of
articles on his plays). From these early beginnings, Bobi Jones's reputation as a critic grew in
parallel with his reputation as a poet. In fact, one
senses that the early criticism was an important
shield with which he protected and nurtured his
own creative drive as poet:

*. . . it is wise for a poet to develop a critical ability to protect
himself from the stifling conservatism of popular aesthetics.
(That's where S. L. and T. S. Eliot come in.)*
(Y FANER, 4 October 1950)

The first book of criticism, I'R ARCH *(Into the Ark)*,
appeared in 1959, a collection of essays on literature and history based on the author's talks with
sixth-form students. Whether we agree or dis-
agree with all the views expressed, we cannot
but be impressed by the book's freshness and
originality. The subjects are arranged in pairs
(like the animals in Noah's ark): the saints and
the Romances; Llywarch Hen and Twm o'r
Nant; Siôn Cent and T. H. Parry-Williams;
DRYCH Y PRIF OESOEDD and Rhys Lewis; O. M.

Edwards and W. J. Gruffydd; the folk tradition
and the tradition of the gentry. In this book we
find some of the features that were to characterize much of the later criticism. First of all, the
book holds our attention—like a discussion, in a
death-camp, on the meaning of being. Without
patronizing dilettantism or sycophantic clichés
(not uncommon in Welsh criticism), it has the
feel of a text that could change our lives. Like
Saunders Lewis's best criticism, it challenges our
own views and presuppositions by offering a
definite point of view.

Alun Llywelyn-Williams, in an appreciative review, mentioned the sense of history that per-
meates all the essays in the book, adding that
Bobi Jones is at his best not when he is generaliz-
ing about various traditions but when he is
discussing individual poets and poems. I'R ARCH
was also reviewed, less favourably but more
influentially, by the dramatist and critic John
Gwilym Jones. In a heated challenge to Bobi
Jones's approach (later reprinted in his
SWYDDOGAETH BEIRNIADAETH), he defended the
rights of a writer to hold any views (pagan or
whatever) without having to be herded into the
believer's ark. Bobi Jones did not hold the simplistic views for which he was criticized, and he
answered John Gwilym Jones in YR ARLOESWR.
John Gwilym Jones's attack showed, however,
that there was an element of misunderstanding,
arising partly, perhaps, from Bobi Jones's highly
enthusiastic, committed stance. In any case, after
publishing I'R ARCH, Bobi Jones was eager to give
the whole theme of his book further careful
consideration.

As we have seen previously, the early sixties was an important period for Bobi Jones because it was then that he developed, or rather discovered, his base in the Calvinistic and evangelical tradition. Alun Llywelyn-Williams had pointed out the evangelical tendency in his review of I'R ARCH. But it was from the early sixties onwards that we see that evangelicalism increasingly informed by a Calvinistic perspective. Bobi Jones (helped by Geoffrey Thomas and others) became acquainted with Christian writers in the Calvinistic tradition such as Abraham Kuyper, Henry R. Van Til, H. R. Rookmaaker, Berkouwer and Dooyeweerd.

After publishing I'R ARCH in 1959, it is perhaps significant that fifteen years went by before Bobi Jones published another major book of criticism. Stating such a fact in these terms, however, may be misleading because he did publish many articles which were later gathered into volumes. Through such articles his critical development was constantly in his readers' view. But he did not rush to commit himself again, without due preparation, in a sizeable *book* of criticism. He took his time (in the midst of a very busy lecturing and publishing schedule) to work out a critical *theory* which would serve as framework, base and guiding authority for all his criticism.

In 1960 he published Y TAIR RHAMANT, a modernized text of the Arthurian legends 'Iarlles y Ffynnon' (or 'Owain'), 'Geraint' and 'Peredur' from *The White Book of Rhydderch* and *The Red Book of Hergest*. Based on his MA thesis, this book showed his enthusiastic concern as teacher of literature that the colourful medieval legends should be made accessible to the ordinary Welsh reader. In this highly productive period in the early 1960s, whilst preparing his Ph.D thesis, as well as two volumes of poetry he published numerous articles and booklets on literature and education, a translation of Rousseau's ÉMILE and his pioneering course for adults learning Welsh.

As researcher and lecturer in the Faculty of Education at Aberystwyth, Bobi Jones's diligent labours, particularly in the field of language revival, produced a wealth of theoretic and practical gains. As a cursory glance at the *Didactic and Applied Linguistics* section at the end of this essay will demonstrate, he made an inspiring contribution in this field. Indeed, his persevering activity, carried out with the help of gifted colleagues—for example in grammatical grading, the emphasis on oral 'drilling', the movement to establish intensive *Ulpan* courses, the two-stream policy of teaching Welsh at both adult and nursery levels, building a model of oral Welsh, Welsh medium education, raising awareness of language restoration in other countries—is a foundational asset to those working in the field of language revival today.

By 1965 he had completed his Ph.D thesis on language development in children (based on his analysis of tape recordings of his daughter Lowri). This study was published in 1970 under the title SYSTEM IN CHILD LANGUAGE and was very favourably reviewed by John Hewson in LANGUAGE. As well as more poetry and collections of short stories, a steady stream of scholarly and literary articles appeared throughout the sixties, and one of his English language contributions from the turbulent close of the decade, HIGH-LIGHTS IN WELSH LITERATURE, is a useful introduction for the non-Welsh-reader to the wealth of Welsh literature throughout the centuries. In the same year, he edited CYFROL DEYRNGED KATE ROBERTS, a collection of articles by various critics dedicated to the renowned *Queen of the Short Story* or, as Bobi Jones had succinctly described her in an article in Y TRAETHODYDD in 1964, *the Suffering Queen.*

This pattern continued during the early 1970s. Then, in 1974, TAFOD Y LLENOR *(The Writer's Tongue)* a major 'post-structuralist study' was published. Nothing quite like this book had appeared in Welsh before. Indeed, it offered a thesis and approach to language and literature which would have been innovative even if it had been published in a majority language such as French or English. The book, which bears the subtitle GWERSI AR THEORI LLENYDDIAETH *(Lessons on the Theory of Literature)*, is divided into five chapters: 'Cyferbyniadau' *(Contrasts)*; 'Ffonoleg' *(Phonology)*; 'Morffoleg' *(Morphology)*; 'Semantoleg' *(Semantology)*; 'Diffinio' *(Definitions)*. As these chapter headings indicate, there is a strong linguistic bias, but the linguistic (and psychological) aspects are constantly applied to literature. The book's genesis goes back to the year Bobi Jones spent in Quebec. It was there that he was introduced to the work of Gustave Guillaume, a linguist who, like Saussure, emphasized the pattern of contrasts which is an integral, basic characteristic of language. Guillaume went further than Saussure by showing that these contrasts bear a sub-conscious dynamic rather than a static relation to each other. Bobi Jones had used this theory in SYSTEM IN CHILD LANGUAGE, and in TAFOD Y LLENOR he extended the theory to the domain of literature. As he explains in the introduction, his aim is to inquire into the *genesis* of a work of literature, *the central process of turning language into literature*. His task is similar to describing grammar, and the grammar that he is most interested in is the deep one which (*à la* Guillaume) asks questions about the meaning of the basic framework which is the basis for all the surface classifications of all languages. *Literature has something to teach to linguistics, and linguistics has something to teach to those who study literature.* Since the language itself is a system, he explains, one can draw the conclusion *that creating literature (i.e. turning language into literature) is an extra system within or around the system which already exists.*

TAFOD Y LLENOR, which preceded studies from the same perspective in other languages (although it used the previous findings of formalists such as Roman Jakobson), did not receive its due appreciation in Welsh—a reminder of the disadvantages of publishing scholarly and original studies in a minority language. One of the few Welsh readers who were sufficiently endowed to understand and appreciate the work was Professor J. E. Caerwyn Williams to whom we should be grateful for providing the sort of knowledgeable feedback that encouraged his colleague to continue his original studies in literature. As Bobi Jones explained in his interview with him, his ambition in TAFOD Y LLENOR had been to study the scientific structure of literature, a similar undertaking to John Morris-Jones's CERDD DAFOD. Another field of interest was the task of defining a Welsh aesthetics (in a similar vein to Saunders Lewis's famous approach to Dafydd Nanmor) and examining the aims of literature. His studies in this area lead to the publication, in 1977, of LLÊN CYMRU A CHREFYDD (*Welsh Literature and Religion*). In 1975, between these major studies, another large book of criticism was published—LLENYDDIAETH GYMRAEG 1936–72 (*Welsh Literature 1936–72*), a work to which he used to refer, with a smile, as his 'popular' book. This is a detailed study of the work of about sixty contemporary authors, mostly based on articles which had first appeared in BARN and Y TRAETH-ODYDD. The various chapters cohere to create a unified whole through the medium of the author's lively and informed, critical perception. The book, which was reviewed appreciatively by Dr Emrys Parry and Professor Derec Llwyd Morgan, highlights the wealth of Welsh litera-ture in a period which had often been unfavour-ably compared to the halcyon days of the older generation. Without being flattering or dis-ingenuous, the approach is both tough and encouraging. Part of the book's main interest is the oblique light it shines on the work of Bobi Jones himself because, although he does not mention his own work, we know that many of the authors under his searchlight were his con-temporaries and compatriots.

LLÊN CYMRU A CHREFYDD is, in many respects, Bobi Jones's most significant and interesting

critical study within the sphere of the Welsh
tradition. It was *his most important contribution in the
field of literary criticism* as the *Oxford Companion to the
Literature of Wales* claimed. Already, in 1971, he had
published Sioc o'r Gofod, a collection of essays
on 'historical Christianity' written from a committed religious viewpoint. In Llên Cymru a
Chrefydd he examined Welsh literature, from its
beginnings to the contemporary period, from the
same Calvinistic perspective. As in the earlier
I'r Arch, literature is discussed with great
ardency. It is something that matters, and not
mere entertainment—something that has the
potential to change our lives. Euros Bowen
argued in a review that the book was incorrect
to claim that the main Welsh tradition was
Augustinian and Calvinistic. Certainly, Euros
Bowen's review contained Arminian statements,
and many other modern Welsh authors would
hold similar Arminian beliefs. Some Welsh
writers hold agnostic or even atheistic beliefs,
but this does not invalidate the analysis of the
tradition which Bobi Jones offers. He sees the
wealth of (mostly religious) literature in our
past in a clear historical, theological and philosophical light. Insights gained from his reading
not only in Welsh literature but also in contemporary Reformed studies such as Henry R. Van
Til's Calvinistic Concept of Culture abound.
(Geoffrey Thomas, who studied under Dr
Cornelius Van Til in Westminster Seminary in
Philadelphia, was the person who introduced
Bobi Jones to the work of the two Van Tils and
other Reformed writers.) Llên Cymru a
Chrefydd, however, is not restricted to Christian
Reformed writings: as always in Bobi Jones's

works of criticism, there is a backdrop of wide
reading in the world's great literatures, past and
present. One does not have to share his religious
belief to appreciate that his study offers a fertile
ground for meditating upon some of the most
central themes and issues that have exercised the
minds of the world's great writers in all ages.
His approach, although steeped in the Augustinian and Calvinistic tradition, does not ignore
the problems of a modern world where the old
certainties are questioned. On the contrary, he
is empathically aware of the difficulties which
face the modern writer in a century which has
specialized in godless philosophies. But he is not
afraid to face such philosophies head-on. This
does not mean that he has neat and ready
answers for all problems (for example for the
nihilist's despair as revealed in modern literature) but it does mean that he has the confidence to perceive those problems in a Christian
perspective and to show that such a perspective
is extremely relevant—to life and literature—
even when it is rejected.

Some of the issues discussed in Llên Cymru a
Chrefydd—in the long introduction for instance
—might appear, at first sight, to be rather ab-
stract and remote from literature. There is a
closer look at individual authors and their work
in later sections of the book (and in other
volumes of criticism). But the most lively and
gripping sections of this study are those where
the author's Calvinistic *Weltanschauung*—his philosophy of life and literature—faces the more
common humanistic *Weltanschauung* of modern
authors and critics. The Reformed critique of

modern humanism—with its apparent optimism which inevitably reverts to underlying pessimism —is seen in action in the case-study milieu of Welsh literature. The chapters which deal with individual Christian authors of the past, like Morgan Llwyd, William Williams Pantycelyn and Gwilym Hiraethog, help us to appreciate the wealth of Christian literature which has been produced in Wales. The book as a whole offers a fascinating insight into the possibilities of a literature and culture which are firmly based in Christian belief; without overlooking the 'pietistic' danger, it gives us a glimpse of the cultural landscape of the new creation.

Professor R. Tudur Jones, in his review of Llên Cymru a Chrefydd (in Bwletin Diwinyddol 2, August 1978), described it as *the most important book on Welsh culture to have been published since the Second World War* ... *It is important to realize that Dr Jones is not saying that writers who accept a theological standpoint similar to his own are to be commended and the rest to be scorned* ... *His basic conviction on this matter is that God's general grace upholds people to create fine literature* ... *whatever their belief.* The reviewer then proceeded to place the book and its author in their theological context—in the balanced Calvinistic school of Abraham Kuyper and similar Reformed scholars.

After the publication of Llên Cymru a Chrefydd, as always, there was a steady stream of articles in the various periodicals. A booklet on Ann Griffiths appeared in 1977. The readers of Y Cylchgrawn Efengylaidd *(The Evangelical Magazine)* found his numerous articles published in that magazine helpful as guidelines to face up to, on the one hand, an increasingly agnostic and secularized Wales, and, on the other, a pietistic tradition which looked askance at all vigorous and industrious cultural and political activities.

Some of the most important aspects of Bobi Jones's contributions in the field of literary criticism are seen in his pioneering four-volume study SEILIAU BEIRNIADAETH *(The Foundations of Criticism)*, published between 1984 and 1988. In these volumes we see a further development of the ideas which were propounded in TAFOD Y LLENOR. Yet, of all his literary studies, SEILIAU BEIRNIADAETH is probably his most original and brilliant contribution to date.

The volumes present a post-structuralist study, an attempt to explore one major aspect of litera-ture—the unseen forms which, it is argued, lie at the root of all literature. To do justice to these volumes would require a separate study. It is imperative to realize that their central theme is not *mynegiant (expression)* but *tafod (langue)*. What the author means by *tafod (tongue)* is 'a sort of Platonism' regarding the very general forms that seem to occur in all Indo-European literatures (at least), but which take particular and charac-teristic structures in their various linguistic traditions. Thus, the great general forms such as metre, rhyme, metaphor, metonymy, irony, parallelism, lyric, drama, story and so on crop up in different literatures in various ways. They require therefore analysis and explanation not only of their permanent potential core shape, and of the reasons for their 'being', but also of

106

the different ways literary traditions discover or
mould them. So too do their individual and
diverse expression in particular works, expression
in action conditioned by 'tongue', yet nevertheless possessing its own effect and context. Bobi
Jones's analysis of the forms of literature extends
the linguistic ideas of Gustave Guillaume,
demonstrating the movement of the mind as it
departs from the literary systems in 'tongue'
(similar to linguistic systems such as the three
persons of the pronoun or the tenses of the verb)
and proceeds to diverse and infinitely varying
expressions in creative works. As mentioned
earlier, Guillaume's 'dynamic' theory of language had already been applied in SYSTEM IN
CHILD LANGUAGE. In SEILIAU BEIRNIADAETH, as in
TAFOD Y LLENOR, his theory is applied—in a highly
original manner—to literature. The basic patterns that Guillaume found in language (simple
contrasts such as absence/presence) are traced
also in literature. Thus SEILIAU BEIRNIADAETH is
an extremely ambitious study analysing not only
the roots of Welsh literature but also the roots of
all literatures in the Indo-European languages.
The approach, however, though it has wide
application is precise and scientific. Although
there is a general and philosophical aspect to
these studies, they offer fascinating insights into
the practical details of artistic creation.

In the first volume, 'Rhagarweiniad' (Preface), it
is argued that literary criticism should not be
confined to impressionistic essays of biography
and appreciation. There is a scientific approach
which looks in depth at the inner dynamic
structures of literary creation, and we should not

be afraid of this scientific approach which employs some of the vocabulary of classical literary criticism. It is argued that *a science of literary criticism is possible; and its task is to explore the deepest initial forms.*

Such concepts as variety within unity are applied to show the rich variety (of life and literature) which should be reflected in a complete and balanced critical theory. Behind the variety, the author finds the basic elements *à la* Guillaume. This concept is comparable to the 'standard model' which physicists use to explain both the nature of matter and the forces which govern it, a model which has led to recent experiments which show that there are only three families of fundamental particles. Like modern physicists, Bobi Jones also perceives, at the heart of life and literature's complexities, certain fundamental and basic patterns.

*Language has been built on the presupposition or perception that there is a basic order behind all apparent chaos. Behind the complex variety there are governing forms . . . Language cannot be used—even to describe what is considered to be chaos—without essentially accepting that order is a prerequisite . . . Likewise, literature is impossible without order. This is presupposed by the literary critic; this is also the writer's presupposition.*

(Vol. 1, pp. 22–3)

In the last chapter of the first volume it is argued that a complete theory of criticism should have sufficient scope and depth to include all the various aspects found in life and literature.

In the second volume, 'Ffurfiau Seiniol' *(Auditory*

*Forms*), the author analyses in greater depth some of the aspects of poetic craft which were discussed in John Morris-Jones's CERDD DAFOD. The discussion is necessarily detailed and technical, but the chapters are full of informative examples from the poetic tradition and are relevant to practising poets as well as literary critics.

In the third volume, 'Ffurfiau Ystyrol' *(Meaning in Forms)*, there is an original and persuasive use of the classical critical vocabulary in a contemporary setting. In the fifth chapter, which deals with *Coegi (Irony)*, Bobi Jones analyses the detailed structures of irony in the context of general trends in current sensibility. In this magisterial chapter, he argues that elements of irony are a constructive contribution but that in much modern literature the bias towards irony is too pronounced and destructive.

In the fourth volume, 'Cyfanweithiau Llenyddol' *(Literary Genres)*, the aim again, as explained in the preface, is not to present a superficial description of external examples only, but to delve into the central crux of basic principles.

The four-volumes of SEILIAU BEIRNIADAETH were reviewed by Dr Ioan Williams in LLAIS LLYFRAU (October 1989) and certain strands in the review were pursued further by Bobi Jones in BARDDAS 152–3 December/January 1989–90.

One of the most demanding aspects of these discussions is the philosophical development of ideas. As is usually the case with original philosophical discussions, time must be taken to become acquainted with the author's vocabulary, definitions and diction before his arguments can be appreciated in full. These volumes deserve the prolonged and hard study which has been given to the work of original thinkers in the field of ideas and literature. Their influence—on critics and writers of creative literature—could be profound.

One of the strengths of Bobi Jones's critical approach is its integral variety. Numerous examples come to mind from his many volumes of criticism where light is shed on particular works of literature and where our critical enjoyment and appreciation of literature are enhanced.

That is certainly true of LLENYDDIAETH GYMRAEG 1902–1936, a companion volume, published in 1987, to the earlier LLENYDDIAETH GYMRAEG 1936–1972. One cannot but be impressed by the immense scope of the work. Here, in a hefty volume of 581 pages and 51 chapters, the focus once more is on particular authors and particular works of literature. There are seven chapters which concentrate on literary forms such as the lyric and the short story. This is a book to which we can return again and again to savour what Bobi Jones has to say about the generation of W. J. Gruffydd and T. H. Parry-Williams, and others. His tone, though sometimes sharp, is considerate and appreciative and hardly ever dull. When he was young, the attitude of the older generation towards him was (generally) rather negative. A milder, less stubborn personality might have been forever silenced. Not so Bobi Jones. He showed the way for writers of his own generation to refute their older critics and speak with their own voice. But it is to his credit that, when he too could speak with the respected authority of a professor of Welsh, he did not deride the efforts of those who had tilled these fields before him. Neither did he follow the bad example of those amongst them who had looked down rather loftily at the efforts of the younger generation. On the contrary he makes a conscious effort to appreciate and encourage the work of young critics and poets—particularly where he sees the danger of the language losing a talented voice.

LLENYDDIAETH GYMRAEG 1902–1936 makes fascinating reading. It re-creates those formative years in modern Welsh literature which have often been described as a renaissance period. Again we notice the hard edge to Bobi Jones's critical prose. His critical perception is constantly awake as he shows the strengths and weaknesses of respected literary figures such as John Morris-Jones and R. Williams Parry, and even when he discusses the life and work of his early hero, Emrys ap Iwan, he does so with a remarkable degree of clear-sighted objectivity. Like Emrys ap Iwan, Bobi Jones has the ability of all great critics to see things as they are and to concentrate the attention of his readers on the central issues.

To conclude: we have sketched, in outline, Bobi Jones's life and literary career. Inevitably, in a short study there are many avenues which could not be followed. Much more could have been written on each aspect of his work. And there are particular works or aspects which have not even been touched upon. For instance, a complete study could be dedicated to the lively philosophical argument between Professor Bobi Jones and Professor Dewi Z. Phillips. In such an argument we see the clash between two value-systems. One senses that it is difficult for someone who is committed to the liberal humanist tradition to appreciate the radically different outlook of a committed Calvinist like Bobi Jones. It is interesting that a modern philosopher of religion like Dewi Z. Phillips finds little to commend in the eulogistic stance of Bobi Jones (as opposed to an agnostic or questioning stance). It is also, perhaps, ironic that here in Wales, where we have such a rich Augustinian, Calvinistic and eulogistic heritage—seen, for instance, in Bobi Jones's PEDWAR EMYNYDD *(Four Hymnists)* (1970) and his BLODEUGERDD BARDDAS O'R BEDWAREDD GANRIF AR BYMTHEG *(Barddas Anthology of Nineteenth Century Verse)* (1988)—it should appear that it is one of the most outstanding heirs of that tradition who is in the minority.

We have seen that Bobi Jones came from a largely Anglicized Welsh background. Is it conceivable that he could have joined the ranks of the 'Anglo-Welsh' writers? This would be a difficult claim to substantiate without ignoring Bobi Jones's published standpoint on the matter (for example in PLANET 42, April 1978). In another article in PLANET, under the title 'Why I Write in Welsh' (PLANET 2, November 1970), he has explained that, to a large extent, he had little choice as to which language he had to use:

*Writing in English or any other foreign language is, for me,*

112

*a discipline, necessary but almost tedious and irrelevant. I still can't help savouring the salty tang of a Welsh which will always be for me a new-old language ... Why I write in Welsh is partly why I write at all ...*

We have followed his prolific career as poet, writer of creative prose and literary criticism. In a period when many writers have taken a minimalist approach, he has resolutely taken the maximalist highroad. Having examined all too briefly some of his most brilliant achievements, much remains unsaid. Together with front-rank Welsh academics like Professor R. Geraint Gruffydd and Professor R. Tudur Jones, he has let the salt and light of his Christian conviction influence his work and outlook in both life and literature. Will Wales, one day, fully appreciate his leadership in the difficult field of reviving the language? If so, what will future generations have to say about his work? They will certainly be grateful. Today, as in his younger days, Bobi Jones is not unaccustomed to facing opposition and even derision at times. But, with his own particular stubborn brand of realistic Christian optimism, he has not buckled under to the strongest attacks. In a period in our history when the language and its literature, the Christian faith and the very existence of the Welsh as a people are under constant attack, he has shown the way forward with courage, perseverance and a chuckle in the heart.

# A Selected Bibliography

BOBI JONES

*Poetry*

Y GÂN GYNTAF, Gwasg Aberystwyth, Aberystwyth, 1957.

RHWNG TAF A THAF, Llyfrau'r Dryw, Llandybïe, 1960.

TYRED ALLAN, Llyfrau'r Dryw, Llandybïe, 1965.

MAN GWYN: CANEUON QUEBEC, Llyfrau'r Dryw, Llandybïe, 1965.

YR ŴYL IFORI, Llyfrau'r Dryw, Llandybïe, 1967.

ALLOR WYDN, Llyfrau'r Dryw, Llandybïe, 1971.

GWLAD LLUN, Christopher Davies, Abertawe, 1976.

HUNLLEF ARTHUR: CERDD, Cyhoeddiadau Barddas, Llandybïe, 1986.

CASGLIAD O GERDDI, Cyhoeddiadau Barddas, Llandybïe, 1989.

*Novels*

NID YW DŴR YN PLYGU, Llyfrau'r Dryw, Llandybïe, 1958.

BOD YN WRAIG, Llyfrau'r Dryw, Llandybïe, 1960.

*Stories*

Y DYN NA DDAETH ADREF, Llyfrau'r Dryw, Llandybïe, 1966.

CI WRTH Y DRWS, Llyfrau'r Dryw, Llandybïe, 1968.

DAW'R PASG I BAWB, Llyfrau'r Dryw, Llandybïe, 1969.

TRAED PRYDFERTH, Christopher Davies, Abertawe, 1973.

PWY LADDODD MISS WALES?, Christopher Davies, Abertawe, 1977.

CRIO CHWERTHIN, Cyhoeddiadau Barddas, Llandybïe, 1990.

*Criticism*

I'R ARCH, Llyfrau'r Dryw, Llandybïe, 1959.

LLENYDDIAETH GYMRAEG YN ADDYSG CYMRU, Cyfres yr Academi, 1961.

TAFOD Y LLENOR, Gwasg Prifysgol Cymru, Caerdydd, 1974.

LLENYDDIAETH GYMRAEG 1936–72, Christopher Davies, Abertawe, 1975.

LLÊN CYMRU A CHREFYDD, Christopher Davies, Abertawe, 1977.

ANN GRIFFITHS: Y CYFRINYDD SYLWEDDOL, Llyfrgell Efengylaidd Cymru, Pen-y-bont ar Ogwr, 1977.

SEILIAU BEIRNIADAETH, Cyrol 1–4: Rhagarweiniad; Ffurfiau Seiniol; Ffurfiau Ystyrol; Cyfanweithiau Llenyddol, Coleg Prifysgol Cymru, Aberystwyth, 1984–1988.

LLENYDDIAETH GYMRAEG 1902–1936, Cyhoeddiadau Barddas, Llandybïe, 1987.


*Didactics and Applied Linguistics*

More than forty articles appeared in Yr Athro between September 1962 and December 1966; they (and other important articles by Bobi Jones and his colleagues in this vital field of study) are listed in Helen Prosser, Llyfryddiaeth Dysgu'r Gymraeg yn Ail Iaith 1961–1981, Canolfan Adnoddau Addysg, Coleg Prifysgol Cymru, Aberystwyth, 1985.

ÉMILE, J. J. Rousseau, Cyfieithiad a Rhagymadrodd, Gwasg Prifysgol Cymru, Caerdydd, 1963.

CYFLWYNO'R GYMRAEG (Llawlyfr i Athrawon Ail Iaith), Gwasg Prifysgol Cymru, Caerdydd, 1964.

CYMRAEG I OEDOLION, I & II, Gwasg Prifysgol Cymru, Caerdydd, 1965.

SYSTEM IN CHILD LANGUAGE, University of Wales Press, Cardiff, 1970.

YSGRIFENNU CREADIGOL I FYFYRWYR PRIFYSGOL, Gwasg Prifysgol Cymru, Caerdydd, 1974.

CYFEIRIADUR I'R ATHRO IAITH [co-author with Megan E. Roberts], Part I–III, Gwasg Prifysgol Cymru, Caerdydd, 1974.

GLOYWI IAITH, 1–3, Gwasg Prifysgol Cymru, Caerdydd, 1988.


*Miscellany*

CRWYDRO MÔN, taith, Llyfrau'r Dryw, Llandybïe, 1957.

Y TAIR RHAMANT: [Iarlles y Ffynnon; Peredur; Geraint], Cymdeithas Lyfrau Ceredigion, 1960.

CYFROL DEYRNGED KATE ROBERTS (editor), Gwasg Gee, Dinbych, 1969.

PEDWAR EMYNYDD, Llyfrau'r Dryw, Llandybïe, 1970.

SIOC O'R GOFOD: Ysgrifau am Gristnogaeth
Hanesyddol, Gwasg Gee, Dinbych, 1971.

BLODEUGERDD BARDDAS O'R BEDWAREDD
GANRIF AR BYMTHEG (editor), Cyhoeddiadau
Barddas, 1988.

*Works in English and English Translations*

HIGHLIGHTS IN WELSH LITERATURE, Christopher Davies, Llandybïe, 1969.

'Why I Write in Welsh', PLANET 2, November
1970, 21–5.

'The Last Ditch' [A short story translated by
Elizabeth Edwards], Gwyn Jones and Islwyn
Ffowc Elis (eds.), TWENTY-FIVE WELSH SHORT
STORIES, Oxford University Press, London, 1971.

'I'm your Boy—the four psycho-sociological
positions of the colonised Welshman', PLANET 42
(April 1978), 2–10.

'Welsh Bilingualism: Four Documents', W. F.
Mackey and J. Ornstein (eds.), SOCIOLINGUISTIC
STUDIES: TRENDS IN LINGUISTICS 6, Mouton, 1979,
231–43.

'Mysticism—and a touch of Eastern promise',
FOUNDATIONS, 2, 1979, 38–47.

THE CHRISTIAN HERITAGE OF WELSH
EDUCATION (co-author with Gwyn Davies),
Evangelical Press of Wales & Association of
Christian Teachers of Wales, Bridgend, 1986.

'Narrative Structure in Medieval Welsh Prose Tales', PROCEEDINGS OF THE SEVENTH INTERNATIONAL CONGRESS OF CELTIC STUDIES, Oxford, 1986, 171–98.

THE DRAGON'S PEN: A brief history of Welsh literature (co-author with Gwyn Thomas), Gomer Press, Llandysul, 1986.

SELECTED POEMS, translated by Joseph P. Clancy, Christopher Davies, Llandybïe, 1987.

*Selected Criticism on the work of Bobi Jones*

Waldo Williams, 'Canu Bobi Jones' [a review of Y GÂN GYNTAF], LLEUFER, Vol. 13, 1957.

R. Gerallt Jones, 'Gŵr Gwadd: Bobi Jones', YR ARLOESWR, no. 7, 1960.

Pennar Davies, 'Cerddi diweddar Dr Bobi Jones', Y GENHINEN, vol. 17, 1966–7, 15–19.

Bryan Martin Davies, 'The Poetry of Bobi Jones', POETRY WALES, vol. 8, no. 1, 1972, 3–16.

Derec Llwyd Morgan, 'R. M. Jones (Bobi Jones)', BARN, 148, May 1975, 649–51.

R. Tudur Jones, 'Adolygiad' [a review of LLÊN CYMRU A CHREFYDD], BWLETIN DIWINYDDOL, No. 2, August 1978, 19–22.

Gwyn Thomas, 'Traeth y De', DADANSODDI 14, Gwasg Gomer, Llandysul, 1984, 78–83.

Meic Stephens (ed.), 'Robert Maynard Jones', THE OXFORD COMPANION TO THE LITERATURE OF WALES, Oxford University Press, 1986, 321–2.

Alan Llwyd, BARDDONIAETH Y CHWEDEGAU, Cyhoeddiadau Barddas, 1986, 468–93; 574–98.

Joseph P. Clancy, 'Beyond Irony: The Poetry of Bobi Jones', BOOK NEWS, Spring 1987, 3–4.

R. Geraint Gruffydd, 'Tu hwnt i amau y mae dinas wen' [Comments on HUNLLEF ARTHUR], BARDDAS, 123/4, July/August 1897, 32.

J. E. Caerwyn Williams, 'Cyfres Chwyldroadol' [A review of SEILIAU BEIRNIADAETH], BARDDAS, 142, February 1989, 14–16.

*Interviews*

Waldo Williams, 'Sgwrs gyda Bobi Jones' [A conversation with Bobi Jones], YR ARLOESWR, January 1958. Reprinted in Robert Rhys (ed.), WALDO WILLIAMS: CYFRES Y MEISTRI 2, Christopher Davies, Abertawe, 1981, 120–6.

J. E. Caerwyn Williams (ed.), 'Bobi Jones yn Ateb Cwestiynau'r Golygydd' [Bobi Jones answers the editor's questions], YSGRIFAU BEIRNIADOL IX, Gwasg Gee, Dinbych, 1976, 376–407.

Alan Llwyd (ed.), 'Cyfweliad gyda Bobi Jones ar achlysur cyhoeddi CASGLIAD O GERDDI' [An interview with Alan Llwyd to mark the event of publishing CASGLIAD O GERDDI], BARDDAS, 147–8, July/August 1989, 6–9.

# Acknowledgements

Grateful acknowledgements are due to the following:

Professor Joseph P. Clancy (whose translations in BOBI JONES: SELECTED POEMS, Christopher Davies, 1987, were used whenever possible); the BBC's Radio Cymru; James Eirian Davies; Siôn Meredith; Dafydd Alwyn Owen; Meic Stephens; Geoffrey Thomas; Dr Huw Walters; Paul Williams; the University of Wales Press.

Last but not least I would like to thank Professor Bobi Jones for providing answers to my questions and for his kind permission in allowing me to quote from his publications, in particular his CASGLIAD O GERDDI and SELECTED POEMS.

# The Author

John Emyr was born in 1950 in Llanwnda near Caernarfon but spent most of his childhood in Rhyl where he attended the pioneering Welsh School, Ysgol Glan Clwyd. He was then educated at the University College of Wales, Aberystwyth. He taught Welsh and English at Ysgol David Hughes, Menai Bridge, and was then Head of the Welsh Departments at Ysgol Aberconwy and Ysgol Friars, Bangor. Since 1988 he has been the General Editor at the Language Studies Centre, Bangor. He has published novels, short stories (MYNYDD GWAITH), poetry and criticism. He was awarded an MA degree for his critical study of the later work of Kate Roberts; he won the Ellis Griffith memorial prize for his book ENAID CLWYFUS which was based on that study. He has edited the works of Lewis Valentine, DYDDIADUR MILWR, and a book of Christian poetry, O GYLCH Y GAIR. He now lives in Bangor with his wife and their two children.

*This Edition,*
*designed by Jeff Clements,*
*is set in Monotype Spectrum 12 Didot on 13 point*
*and printed on Basingwerk Parchment by*
*Qualitex Printing Limited, Cardiff*

*It is limited to 1000 copies of which this is*

*Copy No.*   0407

*British Library Cataloguing in Publication Data*

Emyr, John
    Bobi Jones.—(Writers of Wales).
    1. Welsh literature. Jones, Bobi, 1929–
    I. Title    II. Series
    891.668209

    ISBN 0-7083-1101-6